FEARLESS
GOLF

doubleday

new york london toronto sydney auckland

FEARLESS GOLF

GOLF

conquering the mental game

Dr. Gio Valiante
with Mike Stachura

A GOLF DIGEST BOOK

PUBLISHED BY DOUBLEDAY
a division of Random House, Inc.

DOUBLEDAY and the portrayal of an anchor with a dolphin are
registered trademarks of Random House, Inc.

Book design by Rachel Reiss

Library of Congress Cataloging-in-Publication Data
has been applied for.

ISBN 0-385-51192-2

PRINTED IN THE UNITED STATES OF AMERICA

June 2005

9   10

This book is dedicated to my father, Fred Valiante, for always teaching me that golf, at its core, is a *human* game.

And to my mother, Joanne Valiante, for the endless and unconditional love and encouragement.

And finally, to Professor Frank Pajares. Thank you for the wheat fields.

contents

acknowledgments

It has been a genuine privilege to work with Jason Kaufman, Bob Carney, Mike Stachura, Jenny Choi, and all the folks at *Golf Digest* and Doubleday. They are models of dedication and professional excellence.

I'd like to give thanks to a number of people who helped make this book possible. To the golfers who were so generous with their time during the early days of this study: Buddy Alexander, Joan Alexander, Jonathan Byrd, Chad Campbell, Stewart Cink, Chris DiMarco, David Duval, Luke Donald, Ernie Els, Steve Flesch, Matt Kuchar, Justin Leonard, Davis Love III, Josh McCumber, Bryce Molder, Gary Nicklaus, Jack Nicklaus, Mark Omeara, Gary Player, Nick Price, Heath Slocum, Curtis Strange, and Scott Verplank. You didn't need to help, and you did anyway. That speaks volumes.

Tom Fazio believed in me and my ideas, and gave me the break I needed in order to do this study. He is an exemplary professional, philanthropist, human being, and father.

Wendy Brandon, Roger Casey, Linda Deture, Scott

Hewit, Madeline Kovarik, Al Moe, Deb Wellman, and all my colleagues at Rollins College encourage and model excellence every single day. Hogan advised that we should all "dine with good putters." That's what I do with you!

Personal experience is as great a teacher as research. I've learned many lessons on being a fearless winner from Fran Hoxie, John Bartell, Brian Cleary, Mike Bison, Jen Crane, Beth Cranston and her father General Stewart Cranston, Professor Jack McDowell, Dino Doyle, Brian Froehling, Mike Grieder, Scott Hayward, Jocelyn Hoffman, Chris Aden, Dave and Mary Houle, Brian Kaineg, Steve Losardo, John and Beth Lynn, Bob Mezzo, Jeremy Moore, Adam Sehnert, John Mudry, Cory Nichols, Matt Orrell, Shane and Katie Perkey, Rick Plasky, Joe Sora, Tyrus Underwood, and Walt Rivenbark.

Some relationships transcend words. The friends who shape me and fashion my mind, and who model ethics, character, and excellence every day, are Christian Hoffman, Eric Mudry, and John Black. Gentlemen, thank you!

Golf is a human game. We all play together.

FEARLESS
GOLF

Golf's Greatest Moments

Think of the great moments in golf.

Think of Ben Hogan at Merion in 1950, just sixteen months from a horrific car crash that nearly took his life and left his legs too weak to resume a full tournament schedule. On the final 36-hole day of the U.S. Open that year, Hogan faced a stunningly difficult 1-iron shot from the fairway uphill to the green on the long par 4 finishing hole. The great champion, whose weary legs barely held him up through the final 18 holes, made as majestically precise a swing as the game has ever seen at that crucial moment, and his textbook par propelled him into a playoff he would win the next day. At the moment of truth, Hogan was determined, resolute, and unfazed. He was, in a word, fearless. "The view I take of this shot is markedly different from the view most spectators seem to have formed," Hogan later wrote in his definitive instruction book, *The Modern Fundamentals of Golf*:

> They are inclined to glamorize the actual shot since it was hit in a pressureful situation. They tend to think of it as something unique in itself, something almost inspired, you might say, since the shot was just what the occasion called for. I don't see it that way at all. I didn't hit that shot then—that late afternoon at Merion. I'd been practicing that shot since I was 12 years old. After all, the point of tournament golf is to get command of a swing which, the more pressure you put on it, the better it works.

Think of Jack Nicklaus, seemingly well past his prime at age forty-six, striding the fairways of Augusta National on the final day of the 1986 Masters with a renewed vigor and focus and passion. With others around him doubting his chances, Nicklaus was driven by a consuming belief in his potential, and he would not be denied. He rallied from 5 strokes off the lead to win his sixth green jacket, fearlessly charging to the lead with a back nine 30 while other, younger players faded in the final-round pressure. In the heat of that great moment, Nicklaus was relentless, sure, and focused. He, too, was fearless. "This was Sunday at the Masters," Nicklaus said that victorious evening. "There's a lot of pressure. The other guys feel it, too. They can make mistakes. I knew if I kept my composure down the stretch, as long as I kept making birdies, I'd be OK. I kept that right at the front of my mind. . . . I told my son Jackie, my caddie, at the seventeenth that this was the most fun I've had in five or six years."

Think of Tiger Woods in 2000, when the game's next great player seemed at his invincible best. Yet at the PGA Championship at Valhalla that August he was matched stride for stride by Bob May, an unheralded, unruffled veteran who had never won a PGA Tour event. On the verge of the greatest year in the history of professional golf, Woods had everything to lose, yet he refused to wilt on the biggest stage in the biggest moment. Staring at an unsettling, sliding putt on the eighteenth green, knowing May had just made another birdie and knowing a miss would mean defeat, Woods faced elimination stout and strong and undaunted. He, like Hogan and like Nicklaus, also was fearless. "You have to reach deep inside yourself and you have to keep making birdies," he said. "We never backed off from one another. Birdie for birdie and shot for shot, we were going right at each other. That was just so much fun. That's as good as it gets right there."

When I turn my critical eye on all these great moments, there is one thing the great champions manage to overcome. It is a greater foe than any apparently invincible opponent, than any brutally penal golf course itself or even the unshakable enormity of any once-in-a-lifetime moment. It is fear, the most critical impediment to playing golf to your greatest potential. It matters not if you are a weekend hacker in the later stages of your usual Saturday game or a PGA Tour champion stepping to the eighteenth tee with a one-shot lead. If there is one universal truth to golfers of all levels, it is fear, fear of failure, fear of embarrassment, fear of the unexpected, fear of poor judgment. It is fear of long courses, of short courses, of narrow courses, of hilly courses and flat courses. It is fear of water hazards and sand bunkers, of short putts and long putts. We even fear things that in reality aren't there, like that flagstick that looks to be inches beyond a bunker when it's really a dozen or more yards.

It is fear of playing with certain people or against certain people or even in front of certain people. It is even fear of knowing we are afraid, and it gnaws on our consciousness, undermines our skills, sabotages our capabilities, and infects our confidence.

So let me be clear and succinct on the foundation of this book: A golfer's greatest enemy is fear, but playing our greatest golf begins by making fearless swings at specific targets, regardless of the circumstances. In the simplest terms, *the greatest golfers play fearless golf.*

The lessons I have learned from studying the great players of years past as well as today's emerging greats are varied and complex, yet I can summarize them simply. What golfers of all abilities must come to see is that maximizing your potential in golf begins and ends with one requirement: You must learn to effectively deal with fear, to embrace its challenge to your skills and to overpower it so you can think clearly and effectively and play your best. Anything less invites the insidious decay of doubt and inconsistency. It is what Bobby Jones once called "the one kind of confidence that everyone must have in abundance." His words from seventy-five years ago are as true as they are elegantly written, and they are a beacon for the rest of this book:

> There are many men who play golf exceptionally well when the issues are small, but who collapse when anything of importance is at stake. What causes the detonation is fear—lack of confidence in the swing—making them unwilling to trust it with anything that really matters. In the face of such an obstacle, tension takes the place of relaxation and strain upsets rhythm. The smoothest machine in the world cannot run in a bearing full of the gravel of uncertainty.
>
> When a man stands up to the ball ready to make a decisive stroke, he must know that he can make it. He must not be afraid to swing, afraid to pivot, afraid to hit; there must be a good swing with plenty of confidence to let it loose.

fear and you

Do you remember the first time you drove a car? Undoubtedly, you were excited. Most likely, the act of driving a car wasn't foreign to you. You had been pretending for years: You'd spent time driving pretend race cars and tooling around in the bumper car ring at the local amusement park.

You'd played video games that simulated the steering and shifting motions and the driver's-eye view of oncoming traffic. And, of course, you'd probably sat in a parent's lap and steered the family car in the driveway when you were a youngster. Now, however, that parent was sitting to your right, in the passenger seat, and you alone were in control of the vehicle. All two tons of metal on the open road rested in your untested hands. In an instant, any excitement was tempered by uncertainty, hesitation, confusion. As the car lurched forward, you mashed on brakes or overcorrected a turn. As cars approached from the opposite direction, you slowed to a crawl and hugged the white line on the right edge of the road, no doubt kicking up gravel, to the consternation of mom or dad in the seat next to you. Though in another setting, in front of a video monitor or with the car sitting in the driveway, you were calm, comfortable, and in control, here, now, it was as if the car was some kind of rabid animal on the verge of plunging into a death spiral.

Now, think about the last time you drove a car. If you are like most people, you probably made a phone call or two, adjusted the heating or air conditioning, and changed stations or CDs on the car stereo several times. You steered the wheel effortlessly with just one hand, or maybe with only a couple of fingers, or perhaps even just with your knees. You hardly noticed oncoming traffic, and if you did it might be only to admire another driver's new Lexus or BMW or Mercedes. You believed you were in complete control of this hulking two tons of steel, even at speeds well over seventy miles per hour.

So, what was at the root of the difference between that first driving experience and the last? What was present in the first session that wasn't there in the last? That's simple. It's what I consider to be the most destructive force in any human endeavor: fear. Fear confuses us, limits us, and causes us to achieve less than our abilities otherwise would allow. It blocks us, and with each successive failure, it gathers strength like a virulent disease.

Now, what happened to improve the last time at the wheel over the first? Experience, namely, the kind of experience that breeds calm, comfort, and confidence. If fear is the great enemy, its undefeated conqueror is confidence. Confidence does not ignore fear, it overcomes fear. Confidence starts with knowledge, understanding, and accomplishment. As skill develops, so too does the potential for confidence. Each time we move past fear, we increase the likelihood for success. Confidence strengthens our resolve, even when success is not immediate. Confidence builds on itself, each new experience is fueled by the last and then goes on to fuel the next.

The sports psychology of golf, the mental approach to success in the game, is all about this struggle between fear and confidence. Ben Hogan once was asked to describe golf in a single word. "Sideways," was his answer. It was a remarkably perfect assessment in its simplicity. If I were asked to describe the aim of successful thinking in golf, my answer would be just as simple and just as direct. That one word is "Fearless."

I believe that if there is one universal experience golfers of all levels encounter, it is fear. It doesn't matter whether you are trying to win a major championship, playing in the first round of a club championship, teeing off for the first time ever at a company golf outing, standing on the eighteenth tee with a chance to shoot your lowest round ever, or playing a quick nine holes before sundown with a stranger at the local muni— fear looms large in every instance. And it is my belief that the fear the potential major champion faces is in its own way no different and no less destructive than the fear the weekend golfer senses on a quiet Saturday morning.

Fear comes in many forms. We fear failure and ineptitude. We fear embarrassment and the unexpected. We even fear, as Franklin Roosevelt told us, fear itself. We fear who we're playing with, we fear being watched by friends, and we fear being watched by people we don't know and will never meet. Insidiously, fear travels in disguise, largely because we are afraid to admit we are afraid. Only cowards are afraid, and we are afraid of being labeled a coward. We are so attuned to fear that we have become adept at living with it, and learning to hide it from those around us. Laughing and making excuses is easy, much easier indeed than confronting fear on your terms. It hurts to care about anything, so why care?

Of course, we are not so adept at hiding that fear from ourselves. Ultimately, it stands guard, waiting to consume us. That is why I say that a golfer's greatest enemy is not the difficult course or the challenging tournament or the tense situation. No, the golfer's greatest enemy is fear. Every golfer's supreme challenge is to find a way to overcome this basic emotion that, even in the smallest doses, can undermine the soundest mechanical skills.

The successful golfers play fearless golf. It's not that they don't experience fear, because as we've said, fear is natural, inherent in the human condition. Seeing that natural condition and overcoming it through a practical approach to success is the hallmark of fearless golf. As Tiger Woods has offered, fear may be real, but it is no match for the committed, confident golfer. He says, "I refuse to give in to fear, real or imagined, or to be afraid—either consciously or subconsciously—of anything or anyone." It is not enough to know about fear. We must also know how to successfully combat it. There are key psychological principles and factors that enable golfers to overpower their fear so that they can think clearly and effectively and play their best.

Just as you now drive your car fearlessly, so too can you learn to drive, chip, and putt your ball fearlessly. The method for getting there is just as simple. It is about preparation, mental, physical, and emotional. It is understanding the way to approach the game and working to make it uniformly fearless. Ultimately, it is about focus and paying attention to the things that are crucial to success and ignoring those that serve no constructive purpose. For example, it is not unusual to be nervous over an opening tee shot. But thinking about being nervous is a deterrent to success. It does not move you forward toward your goal of making a successful swing. It is "fearful golf" when what success demands is "fearless golf."

Maybe driving a car is a simpler activity than making a golf swing. Of course, a mistake with a car might kill you; a mistake in golf probably won't. We learned to drive with increasing skill every time we got behind the wheel of a vehicle, and along the way, we learned to drive with confidence. That same freedom from fear can inhabit our golf, too. On the following pages, I hope you will learn a little bit of what I have learned over the years in talking with and offering counsel to some of the best golfers in the world. They have taught me much about fear and how to meet it face-to-face. What I have found is that fear in golf is a controllable force. You have to learn to control it or it will find a way to control you at the game's most important moments.

Fear may always exist somewhere in every situation in golf. The challenge is to not let it overwhelm our every move and every thought. Fear is the enemy; confidence is the conquering hero.

CHAPTER 1

Fear Is the Enemy

Jack Nicklaus once wrote that "fear of any kind is the number one enemy of all golfers, regardless of ball-striking and shot-making capabilities. [Fear] happened to me before my early success enabled me to control my fear."

Nicklaus knew fear can take hold of even the most skilled golfers, leaving them not only unable to function to the best of their physical abilities but also dumbstruck by the basic mental mechanics of the game. Nicklaus knew the power of fear from personal experience. It was the 1960 U.S. Open that taught the young Nicklaus the power of fear and the power of focus. He finished second in the U.S. Open that year, a championship many observers believed he might have won. Even Nicklaus admitted he had a chance, until fear got in the way. Leading the tournament by a shot late in the final round, Nicklaus found himself distracted by the moment. On the sixteenth hole, he struck a short birdie putt too boldly after thinking how hard it would be for others to catch him with a two-shot lead. But it got worse for the young champion. Staring at a short par putt with his fellow competitor Ben Hogan standing by, Nicklaus noticed a poorly repaired pitch mark in the line of his putt. He wasn't sure he could repair it under the rules, though he in fact could. In his book *My Most Memorable Shots in the Majors*, Nicklaus wrote:

> Excited, anxious and under as much pressure as I've ever known, I can't focus my mind clearly on whether the rules allow me to repair the ball mark. Also, I'm too shy or embarrassed to admit this in front of Hogan or to hold up play by asking an official. So I go ahead and stroke the putt. The mark deflects the ball just enough to spin it out. I bogey, then three-putt the next green.

Of course, Arnold Palmer won that championship by two shots over Nicklaus, whose fear of the moment shut down his ability to think clearly and act decisively. Fear is a powerful force. It can be destructive, but it can also teach us. As Nicklaus later remarked, "There are three lessons here, which have stuck with me ever since. First: Repair ball marks as you'd like the others to repair them for you. Second: Know the rules. Third: If in doubt, ask."

Now, not many of us have the "early success" of a Jack Nicklaus to help us do battle with the demon of fear on the golf course. But it should be at least slightly comforting that even the most accomplished major champion in the history of the game had at times his own struggles with fear. That is a sure illustration of just how destructive and pervasive fear can be.

In the context of golf, fear is a misplaced and wasted mind activity, but as worthless as it may be, left unchecked it will be crippling to your chances at success. Fear is a termite or a bark beetle or an ascaris worm. It lives inside the host, devouring it from the inside by living on what the host provides. Gruesome, insidious, perhaps, but it's a very effective means of shutting down a system and making it incapable of functioning. That's what happens to the golfer affected by fear. His whole process for shot-making can be turned on its head.

Try this thought experiment: Picture yourself standing on the tee box of a demanding golf hole. Let it be a hole you know well with a water hazard to carry and another down the right side of the fairway. In your mind, picture yourself addressing the ball and looking down the fairway. Visualize the sights, smells, and feel of the moment. Go through your whole preshot routine and setup. Then, just as you are at address and about to hit the ball, ask yourself the following question: "What if I slice?"

What happened? How did you feel the moment after asking yourself that question? Chances are, if you were deeply immersed in this little experiment, and if you are like most golfers, you felt a bolt of anxiety or fear shoot down your spine and maybe even into your stomach and hands. Chances are that you pictured the ball sailing off-line, and your mind filled with dreadful thoughts. In an instant, by asking yourself the simple question, "What if I slice?" you triggered your own anxiety and created your own fear. Excellence in golf requires that you make fearless swings at precise targets. Saying "What if I slice?" does not increase the likely success rate. By asking a bad question, you succumb to fear and put yourself at a disadvantage even before you've taken the club back.

As I've interviewed more and more golfers over the years, I've found that golfers go through a round of golf deep in a conversation with themselves. Sometimes this ongoing dialogue is about swing mechanics (we all remember watching the greats like Nick Faldo or Tiger Woods walking down the fairway making a practice swing trying to isolate a particular move in the downswing). Sometimes the internal conversation is about the golf course and its relative fairness. Sometimes the chatter is about the outcome of the next shot or the way the previous hole finished. The common thread that holds all these topics together is that golfers continually ask questions like these and that these bad questions can be a very destructive influence on the way you score. The fear-filled golfer asks the wrong questions. They are the wrong questions because they elicit a negative emotional reaction. They stall the process of moving toward success, and at their most detrimental actually move the golfer away from success.

Here's a quick lesson in who or what you're playing against: It was the most perfect spring day in a part of the world known for perfect spring days. It was Sunday at the 2002 Heritage of Golf Classic at Harbour Town Golf Links on the beautiful island of Hilton Head, South Carolina. The temperature was a comfortable eighty degrees, there was a soft breeze coming off Calibogue Sound, the fragrant cherry blossoms were in bloom, and golf fans came out by the thousands in their customary southern attire to watch and cheer for the best golfers in the world.

But the poetry and pageantry of the day were lost on the golfers themselves, particularly those in contention to win. For those golfers in the final groups, there was the prospect of a penalizing golf course to deal with. The same Calibogue breezes that were a blessing to the admiring spectators could gust at any moment and send a golf ball flying into the surrounding rough, bunkers, or salt marshes overgrown with sea oats. Standing between each man and victory was a supremely talented group of competitors, each of whom sought his own glory. On this gentle spring day, there were victories to be had, careers to be made, and for those who had left a bit of their soul at Augusta the week before, ghosts to be quieted.

The leaderboard consisted of golf's premier players, including Phil Mickelson, Davis Love III, Billy Andrade, and Heath Slocum. Young Justin Leonard led by three. On the practice range minutes before they were to tee off, Davis Love was committed to catching Justin Leonard: "I'm going to make a run at you!" he joked to his friend Justin. Having never played before a crowd that large, tour rookie Heath Slocum's mind was distracted by the large galleries, and the prospect of playing with the world's number two–ranked player, Phil

Mickelson. Justin Leonard accepted the challenge of protecting the three-shot lead he'd built with the help of a blinding 64 on the second day of the tournament.

On the practice range minutes before he teed off, I put this question to Heath: "If the field is thinking about Justin, and Justin is thinking about his lead, and you are thinking about Phil, who do you suppose is thinking about the golf course?" Heath, whose success on tour was due as much to his quick mind as to his innate talent, immediately understood the point I was trying to make: You cannot play your best golf if your mind is preoccupied with thinking about other golfers. To play your best golf, your mind has to be focused exclusively on hitting shots at precise targets. So, on that glorious day in the spring of 2002, while a handful of golfers on the PGA Tour battled each other, Heath Slocum battled the golf course. And although his run at victory fell a stroke short, of all those in contention on Sunday, he shot the lowest final round score.

A rather unexpected but interesting pattern that emerged from my studies of golfers over the years had to do with the questions of mastery versus ego that golfers asked themselves; different questions that began a mental cycle leading either to fear or fearlessness. Understanding the import of this requires a short lesson on the workings of the mind, beginning with a thought experiment. For this experiment, take a moment and ask yourself four questions. Repeat these questions word for word to yourself and, after each one, pause a moment before moving on to the next:

1. What is the color of my car?
2. What animal produces milk?
3. Who is the best golfer in the world?
4. What are the colors of the American flag?

After reading each question, you no doubt pictured your car, you saw a cow, you pictured Tiger Woods or Jack Nicklaus, and you saw an image of an American flag. In other words, asking yourself questions immediately and powerfully triggered images in your mind. Though simple, this exercise illustrates three foundational mechanisms of human thinking. First, the mind automatically responds to the questions we ask ourselves. Second, the questions we ask ourselves determine where we focus our attention in the sense that, while you were asking those four questions, you were not thinking about politics, the Easter Bunny, or whether your garbage will be picked up on time. And third, the answers to the questions we ask ourselves often come back in visual form. I'd like you to hold on to those key points for the remainder of this chapter.

Certainly, we have all seen how fear makes cowards of us all, as the old expression goes. We all know that fear of public speaking is a tremendously common fear. Poor questions are often responsible for the cold feet that the betrothed feel on their wedding day. A client recently told me of her internal conversation on the morning of her wedding, when unlike anything she had ever done or thought before, she repeatedly asked poor questions of herself like, "What if he stops loving me?" She visualized future misery, and rather than concentrating on the beauty and joy of her wedding day, she was mired in a grip of panic and fear, barely making it through, let alone enjoying, her special day. Surely, we've all experienced a degree of fear of flying. Even though we know that statistically flying is safer than driving, we often can't help but ask ourselves, "What if the plane crashes?" Again, it is not a productive way of thinking. Much like if the mountain climber were suddenly to ask himself, "What if I fall?" Immediately, he is focused on not falling, instead of climbing and enjoying the challenge and the scenery. Self-induced anxiety and fear inhibits positive action.

Fear has its foundation in a focus on the future uncertainties of a particular moment, regardless of how absurd they might be. When you stand on the tee of a tight driving hole and immediately begin to think of a slice or a hook into trouble, why is that any different or more logical than wondering if your plane might crash or if your betrothed will stop loving you or if you will be unable to utter a sound when you have to give that presentation to all the department heads this afternoon? There isn't logic to it, especially if you let yourself fall victim to the cycle of unproductive self-questioning.

Fear begins and gets its fuel from the uncertainty of self-questioning. Most fear-inducing questions boil down to the same theme: What if I am faced with something terrible that I am not prepared for? But go deeper and it is just as easy to realize that this fear can fall away once we are willing to hear an answer to one of these moderately absurd questions. In nearly every case, the answer to a question of uncertainty is a simple, strong, positive question of its own: "What am I going to do about it?" When we ask ourselves "What if the plane crashes?" and we respond with "What am I going to do about it?" we are telling ourselves to look objectively at our particular uncertainty and deal with it thoroughly. In the case of fear of flying, for example, maybe it means reminding ourselves of the safety record of air travel, or even more simply, finding a way to deal with that uncomfortable moment of a flight (takeoff, let's say) by focusing on a process (reading a book, listening to music, closing your eyes and meditating) that takes our mind away from an absurd fear. You will see how that same sort of directed focus can make your next round of golf better, too.

words of a champion: tom kite, u.s. open 1992

Throughout his PGA Tour career, Tom Kite made himself into one of the most consistent performers the game has ever known. He once had twenty-one top tens in a season, and despite having only moderate physical gifts, he rose to number one on the all-time PGA Tour money list in the early 1990s. Kite did it with dedication and an indefatigable desire for improvement. For all that his career encom-

cont. on next page

cont. from previous page

passed, his résumé lacked that one crucial notation: a major championship. Kite shook loose that burden with a gritty performance on one of the toughest days in U.S. Open history. With winds whipping hard around Stillwater Cove and the tiny greens at Pebble Beach the consistency of a parking lot, Kite negotiated his way through 18 tough holes, the forty-mile-per-hour winds, and all the lingering doubters to win his first major title. After lifting the trophy, he said, "From tee to green, it was not even close to one of the best tournaments I've ever had. But as far as hanging in there and doing the things that were required on a very difficult golf course, this may have been the best."

Later, Kite told *Golf Digest* in an extended interview that there's a difference between recognizing fear and being afraid. The nerves will come out, he says, but that's what makes the moment supreme.

The thing that is difficult for people to appreciate is a lot of times when you see a guy that is coming down the stretch trying to win a golf tournament, he looks so calm and so collected and looks like he has everything under control.

They don't understand that the guy who is trying to win a golf tournament out there can look so calm. The guy is not calm. He may look calm and he may have learned how to control his emotions, but I can assure you he is not calm.

No matter how many times you win, the ner-

cont. on next page

cont. from previous page

vousness is there—and it is great. That's the best thing about it, to put yourself in that position and to get nervous, to really get scared. It is what it is all about.

People don't understand how wonderful that feeling is. To absolutely be scared to death that you are not going to be able to perform. And then you do. You pull the shots off—sometimes to your own amazement. It is an incredible feeling. That being scared, that's fun. That's good. If you are not scared, if you don't get that adrenaline pumping, all you can do is average things. I love that. And that is the thing that people don't understand. If you are not scared, it means you don't care.

I constantly remind golfers not to hide from the obstacles that the game throws at them or that their minds try to create. We do not run from obstacles because they will always find us, especially since we cannot run from those within our own minds. So we challenge the obstacles, the fears, by identifying them, learning about them, and understanding how they work against our chances for success.

The first step in fearless golf is to consciously make a decision not to be afraid, or maybe at least to not be afraid of being afraid. We cannot pretend there is no chance of a slice or hook into the trees, but we can set about a process for minimizing the chance for that scenario to play itself out. This is a matter of preparing in advance so that we leave nothing for fear to feed on.

Questions focus our minds in the same way a lens focuses a laser. If Dante was right and the mind can make a heaven of hell or a hell of heaven, then the path to that hell is often paved with terribly absurd questions. Alternatively, the road to heaven (and to successful, fearless golf) is paved with reasonable and effective questions.

A client with whom I worked named Don Snider is a prime example of someone who learned to play through (and with) adversity. Don is an attorney in Boca Raton, Florida, and a fanatical golf fan. He came to me with a common complaint that many golfers face. In important situations he got nervous to the point that he was almost afraid to hit a golf shot. Though he tried everything he could think of to make the fear go away, he simply could not. Sound familiar? Convinced that nervousness was a sure sign of doom, he tended to make bad swings that would kill his score. "If only I could putt under pressure," he said sadly. "Can you teach me how not to be nervous?"

When I explained to Don that all successful golfers on the PGA Tour experience the same feelings, he was incredulous. When I told him that a floppy stomach and tight hands mean only that you are excited and that you should welcome those feelings, he almost asked for a refund. He had come to me hoping I would teach him how to get rid of those thoughts. He hadn't expected that I would suggest to him that he should learn how to play with those thoughts. When our day together ended, he was unconvinced. What follows is an unedited e-mail I recently received from Don:

Hi Dr. Valiante,

I know I am one of your smaller fish, but I am pleased to report that a success story is building and happening!! So many of the things we talked about have really sunk in and helped me. My play continues to be really solid, even under pressure! Possibly, especially under pressure! My attitude has been consistently great for several months now, and I am enjoying the game again. I've had many rounds in the very low 70's, even during some match play competition that I've recently been playing in. I think I'm going to be one of your real success stories. A couple of the specific points working from our time together.

1. *Even on a bad day, I have to come through.*
2. *If I'm nervous, just deal with it, as opposed to trying to make it go away. Whatever demons I have, just deal with them, don't wish them to go away.*
3. *Keep grip pressure consistent during the swing.*
4. *Be a mastery golfer. Always try to hit my good shot; don't think about what I'm trying not to do.*

Don

Don's goal in coming to me had been to learn how not to be nervous. My objective for Don was for him to learn how to hit shots while he was nervous (a strategy that, once mastered, dulls nervousness). As you see, he learned to cope with his nerves. His self-efficacy began to increase dramatically, the fear began to subside, and his golf game and his spirits improved. Oh, and I did charge him.

In terms of processing information, the mind is not much different than an Internet search engine like Google. When a golfer steps to the tee of a difficult hole and at the last moment (or at any moment, really) asks himself, "What if I slice?" he begins a chain reaction that almost instantly dredges up images in the mind's eye of failure, of an undesirable ball flight and of out-of-bounds and penalty strokes. Do these images breed confidence? These images trigger apprehension, disappointment, and uncertainty. This process is the creation of the most destructive force in the golfer's body: fear. That's right, fear isn't merely debilitating from a mental standpoint. It also has a physiological manifestation.

In addition to the inability to concentrate, there can be body tension, loss of sensation in the hands, increased heart rate, dizziness, shortness of breath, sweating, and in extreme cases, nausea, constipation, diarrhea, muscular pain, skin afflictions, and even impotence. No wonder making a decent swing could be the least of your body's concerns the moment it senses fear—even when that fear is entirely self-created. In an instant, by asking a bad question, a golfer can create his own anxiety and undo the confidence required to play this delicate game.

words of a champion: nick faldo

The greatest champions find a way to adapt and they find a way to summon up a new kind of courage at the biggest moments. Nick Faldo had gained the reputation of being a tireless perfectionist, completely rebuilding his golf swing in the mid-1980s and becoming a great champion in the late 1980s and early '90s, but one of his biggest victories came only after all seemed lost. Leading by four shots in the final round of the British Open at Muirfield, Faldo came to the finishing four holes suddenly trailing by two shots. He then summoned his courage and played his best golf of the day right at the exact moment he needed it most, on some of the most demanding finishing holes the game knows. Faldo birdied 15 and 16 with magnificent iron shots and held on for gritty pars on the final two holes, tapping in the final putt through tears. He had learned much about himself in his effort to build a championship swing and develop a new attitude to playing the best he could possibly play. He told reporters later:

I'm not trying to achieve the clinically perfect round of golf. Nor am I lessening my search for perfection. It's just that I'm being less hard on myself when I fail to achieve it.

The point is accepting what is bad and just going on. Learning to be lighter, that really helped.

cont. on next page

cont. from previous page
And when it got the bleakest, trailing late after victory seemed assured starting out, where was his mind? Well, in Faldo's reflections, there's a lesson for those who want to win championships *and* for those who want to break 80 for the first time: "I just told myself, 'It's all gone, just forget it and, for the good, start over. Just forget the whole of the week, what's gone is past. This is the most important part.' It made me feel light again, not heavy."

You see, fear is not simply the product of irrational thinking. Fear is not merely a thought or emotion. In actuality, this physiological response in the body to fear is what's commonly known as the "fight-or-flight" response, inherent in the nervous system of any marginally evolved species. It's the self-preservation instinct that has been part of human makeup since well before man got off all fours and began walking upright. In short, it's part of our DNA. Just as our eyes evolved for seeing and our teeth for chewing, our brain is a biological adaptation designed to promote survival in the environments in which our human ancestors evolved. A brain that evolved to survive in a harsh world had to learn to effectively respond to threats in the environment, and the way the brain effectively responds to threats is with fear. In fact, scientists now understand the anatomy of fear so well that they have named the biological functions and processes "the fear response." An understanding of these processes has important implications for golfers.

Although I have worked to keep this book nontechnical, I believe that the following explanation will be helpful for golfers because to understand the fear response, one first has to understand the different regions of the brain that developed at different times of human evolution. The *cortex*, which is responsible for rational and conscious thought, is a relatively recent evolutionary development. Before the development of the cortex, humans developed the *amygdala*, also known as the fear system's command center. The fear system, governed by the amygdala, is like a throw switch or a fire alarm or a default mechanism that is able to override the conscious mind in large part because the cortex (conscious mind) has few dedicated resources or pathways to influence the fear system, while the fear system has a number of resources to dominate the cortex.

American poet Robert Frost once wrote how poetry "begins with a feeling and finds a thought." His observations are remarkably insightful because the part of the brain (amygdala) that produces feelings such as fear operates far more quickly than the parts of our brains that process "conscious thought" (cortex). We often feel fear before we can think in a rational way about the thing that produced that fear.

words of a champion: ernie els, 2002 british open

Before golfers can master the game, it is essential that they believe that they can do so. Professional golfers who can't get used to the idea of seeing themselves on a leaderboard or winning a major championship are unlikely to perform at championship levels. Ernie Els's goal for the 2002 season was to win at least two of golf's major championships. After conceding the first two to Tiger Woods, Ernie remained resilient in his pursuit of the third. Whereas most golfers are uncomfortable with the thought of winning a major, Ernie was uncomfortable with the thought of *not* winning a major. When he arrived at Muirfield for the British Open, he wanted and expected to win.

He had won two U.S. Opens in his career by the time he arrived at the final round of the 2002 British Open at Muirfield, but he was motivated to achieve more in the game. And yet at the same time, on that fateful Sunday, he was afraid he might never get the opportunity.

Els had entered the final round leading, having survived brutal weather conditions during the third round. He was at the short sixteenth with a one-stroke lead when a poor chip shot led to a double-bogey 5. Down by one now, Els admitted later, "After that I was really almost gone."

But Els composed himself, played the par-5 seventeenth terrifically, and made an easy birdie to get himself into a four-man, 4-hole playoff. The roller-coaster turn of

cont. on next page

cont. from previous page

events wore on Els, who knew he had to stay composed. He had to find a way to fight the fear of losing. That internal struggle made for the greatest victory of his career.

"Walking off 16, a lot of things went through my mind," he said in the press tent afterward. "I was like, 'Is this a way to lose another major, is this the way you want to be remembered, by screwing up an Open Championship?' I'm pretty hard on myself as it is, and that wasn't one of my finer moments."

Before the playoff, Els had time to get himself back in focus. What he said to himself in the intermission allowed him to stare down that growing fear, and as he said later, silence that "little man whispering negative thoughts in your ear."

"I had four holes to play and those four holes were the most important holes of my career and I was going to give it 100 percent on each and every shot. Somehow I pulled myself together and made some good shots again. I guess I've got a little bit of fight in me when it counts."

For instance, when a person sees something threatening such as an aggressive, attacking dog, it takes just a fraction of a second for the amygdala to react. In that fraction of a second, a mixture of chemicals and stress hormones begin bathing the muscles, causing them to tighten. Blood pressure rises, pupils dilate, digestion shuts down, and capillaries constrict, discharging the "fight or flight" response necessary to survival.

Almost a full second later, the cortex receives the message, and the person is able to process the word "dog" and to think in rational terms about the situation. Even at low levels, anxiety causes muscle tension, which in turn can lead to tightness in the golf swing and, even worse for a golfer, flinching muscles and twitching eyes.

Confidence Drill: Eye Test

The eyes betray fear in many ways. The pupils dilate, and the eyes can flinch under pressure. In putting, you will see this manifest itself when a player starts looking down the line before he's actually made a stroke. Maybe you can't eliminate the fear sensation, but what you can do is practice keeping your eyes over the ball well after impact. When I work with players on the putting green, I'll often shield their eyes from looking forward when they practice putting. You could get a playing partner to do the same for you. Another option is to focus on a spot beside the ball, or place a coin right next to the ball and focus on it so you can still read the writing on it after the ball has rolled away. Again, it's not simply the act of not looking at the target before impact. It's the idea of focusing on something that will not be detrimental to your stroke. Keeping your head down and your eyes focused over the ball is simply a better way to execute the putting stroke. Don't think so much of making a good stroke. That should be obvious. Think instead of doing some task, some act that will naturally increase the likelihood of executing a proper stroke. The positive stroke is an aftereffect of this sort of concentration.

There are psychological consequences as well. As information gets routed from the eyes and ears to other parts of the brain for processing, mental stressors come into play. Golfers who "choke" often report being unable to focus. Perception changes, so that those golfers begin to perceive normally innocuous situations as threatening. Where they used to see only fairways and greens, they now see only hazards.

words of a champion: ben curtis, 2003 british open

Ben Curtis was not the name on everybody's lips when the British Open came to Royal St. George's in 2003. Curtis had one career top ten in his PGA Tour career before the 2003 British. Fortunately, it happened to come at the Western Open, where that top ten finish got him into the Open Championship field. Curtis played surprisingly steady for someone who had never played in a major championship of any kind. And while the favorites were falling away, Curtis held on down the stretch, holing a

cont. on next page

cont. from previous page

nervy twelve-foot par putt at the last that eventually would stand up as the winning score.

His thoughts after hoisting the claret jug suggest a golfer who tried very hard to limit his focus to the things he could control, an amazing bit of resolve for the moment of his life.

> I was just in a zone and very focused on what I was doing so much that I didn't really think about winning until afterwards. I've won in the past, just not at this level yet. I was shaking in my boots, obviously, but out there I was just very focused on what I had to do and let my work speak for itself. And if it was good enough, fine. If not, I can live with it.
>
> I was playing hard coming in, and I was trying to keep the course in front of me.

Fear plays tricks on memory as well. The brain has evolved to remember fearful situations so as to be able to avoid them in the future. Many chemicals, such as adrenaline, act like yellow highlighters to ensure the brain remembers fearful situations. Once a fear-causing experience has taken place in our lives, its memory can remain strong and vivid. For example, if you were to get into an automobile accident at an intersection, chances are you would flinch every time you went through an intersection for weeks following the accident. Your brain signals an alarm as it anticipates another crash, even though your conscious mind is aware there isn't a car anywhere in sight. Psychiatrists and clinical psychologists make a pretty penny treating patients with unresolved fears, and in fact I get e-mails weekly from adult golfers who still have vivid, disruptive memories of embarrassing or fearful moments on the golf course that happened to them months and even years before.

This tendency to remember fearful situations can be adaptive in some cases (for instance, remembering the details while walking alone down a dangerous street at night), but in golf these persistent memories become distractive. Just as Hogan admitted to remembering "the negative more vividly than the positive," many competitive golfers who are caught in slumps report that, after a round of golf, they simply cannot remember any good shots. The negative, like cream, rises to the top of their memories.

Golfers who choke even one time often report replaying the episode in their minds over and over again. They can't seem to shake it. Such memories act in the same way as memories of a car crash. They make us frightened when we encounter similar situations. The trickiest problem, of course, is that of *anticipation*. As the old saying goes, Once bitten, twice shy. Past experiences that brought on fear cause us to anticipate similar experiences in similar situations. Anticipating the possibility of missing yet another fairway, a golfer may flinch during his swing. Although psychologists also point out that fear has healthy and adaptive characteristics, few memories are as easy to trigger and hard to shake as those created by fear.

How is it that a sport as innocuous as golf can instigate processes designed to protect us from being eaten in the wild? Well, the mind does not just respond to "actual" threats such as lions, tigers, and snakes. It also responds to "perceived" threats such as embarrassment, disappointment, and frustration. Golfers who learn to fear situations in golf actually condition their minds to perceive situations as more threatening than they really are. They often beat themselves up for making the slightest mistakes, the psychological consequences of which are similar to a car crash. They result in subsequent hesitation, tentativeness, and fear. Thus, by beating themselves up and dwelling on mistakes, golfers engage in a sort of "fear conditioning," by which they can easily learn to perceive the slightest irregularity (a bad bounce, a bad hole, or even a string of good holes) as a warning sign. The fear response goes into effect. Make no mistake about it, fear can be habit forming.

words of a champion: davis love iii, 1997 pga championship

It may have seemed that Davis Love walked onto the PGA Tour in 1986 with the greatest expectations of success, but when he went more than a decade without claiming that first major title, there were doubters, including himself at times. But at the PGA at Winged Foot in 1997,

cont. on next page

cont. from previous page

Love entered the final round poised to win that first major. He had come close several times before, but this particular Sunday he started strong and finished even stronger, birdieing the final hole under a rainbow to win the championship by 5 shots. Coming so close and finally succeeding, the lessons learned by Love are just as applicable to the player on the verge of breaking 80. He told the gathered press that day that part of the difference this time could lie in his having fallen short the times before, that winning the big one

is an inner battle. Obviously, my golf game is good enough to win a major. It is fighting the inner battle that week of, one, getting your golf game ready and then getting your mind there for 72 holes, and controlling the emotions and living through the bad breaks and the good breaks and riding that emotional roller coaster. And I know that you have to be there a few times to understand how to handle it. I mean, I was just as nervous today as I was last year at the U.S. Open. My hands were shaking just as bad, my stomach was churning just as bad. But I reminded myself of what I had to do, to hit the golf ball, to make the putts and keep myself focused, and I got through it. If it wasn't for the times that I haven't won, made the mistakes, and learned from them, I don't think I could have made

cont. on next page

> *cont. from previous page*
>
> it. I could have double-bogeyed those last three
> holes the way I was feeling. But, I played them
> good because I had been there before and lost it
> before and knew what that feeling felt like.

Fear can change your entire perspective, and worse, it insti-
tutes a downward spiral that resupplies its own strength.
Golfers with lower self-confidence (or what we come to know
as "self-efficacy" in later chapters) who interpret physiological
arousal as fear produce more of a stress hormone called *norepinephrine* whose job is to tense the muscles. It is worth reading
that passage again: Norepinephrine tenses the muscles. Every
teacher of the golf swing in the world will tell you that a proper
golf swing cannot be executed with tightness in the muscles.
Tight muscles are not compatible with a relaxed, smooth, flowing, seamless, and full golf swing. In a phrase, the difference between being psyched up or psyched out often has to do with
the meaning we assign to these physiological states. As psychologist Albert Bandura has written, "The difference between
being psyched up or psyched out is a matter of interpretation."
When an event is interpreted as exciting, the body relaxes.
When it is interpreted as frightening, the body tightens.

The cycle commonly known as the "downward spiral"
you see when golfers choke nearly always begins with a dip in
self-efficacy. The spiral goes something like this: Low self-
efficacy results in interpreting physiological change as fear

rather than excitement. Fear feeds on itself and triggers the sympathetic nervous system to do two key things detrimental to golf. First, norepinephrine is produced and muscles tense up. Second, capillaries in the hands constrict, making golfers lose feeling in their hands such that they grip the club really tightly. Tense muscles and tight hands restrict the golf swing, often producing bad shots (jabbed putts or blocked full shots). Bad shots decrease self-efficacy and increase fear, and the cycle simply repeats and insidiously feeds on itself over and over. And there you have it, a psychological breakdown that produces the dreaded downward spiral.

fear and physiology

In my research there are four important and destructive ways that fear impacts the physiology of the golf swing.

Tightening muscles is fine for sports such as football, where all you need to do is hit someone really, really hard. But tight muscles do not work for golfers, whose movements, while forceful, must also be delicate and precise, often all at the same time. The physiological aftereffects of fear influence the golf swing in four distinct ways. Only by knowing these ways can golfers understand how to combat this resulting tightness and make fearless swings at good targets.

Later, we'll talk about how to attack these four problems both from a physical and a mental standpoint.

Problem 1: Golfers' Hands

The first and by far most important way that fear-induced bodily changes influence the golf swing is by altering a golfer's hands. Have you noticed that when people get nervous they fidget with their hands? Anxiety usually makes its first appearance in our hands. When blood flows away from our extremities, the result is that we often lose feeling in our hands. To regain the ability to feel the club in their hands, golfers do what comes naturally—they grip the club tighter. Studies show that golfers who are nervous change their grip pressure equivalent to the amount of tension they feel. The more nervous they become, the tighter they grip the club. Of course, the tighter they grip the club, the more difficult it becomes for the hands to properly follow their path on the downswing. Consequently, even when they are mechanically in all the right positions in the golf swing, the tension in their hands and forearms often kills their timing. This prevents them from releasing the club properly, influencing both distance and direction of their golf shots.

Confidence Drill: Feel the Pressure

As we've seen, the physiologic effects of fear have specific influences on the golf swing. One of the most prominent is that fear alters grip pressure. Because the body's natural fear response causes the blood vessels to constrict, blood is pushed out of the hands. That in turn causes a golfer to grip the club tighter in order to feel the same thing.

But a tighter grip makes it difficult to make a smooth swing with a complete backswing and a full release and follow-through. What you have to learn is to sense when your grip is getting too tight and learn to dial it down.

Try to set up a scale where 1 is the softest hands possible, almost as if you were holding a fragile piece of jewelry or a soap bubble on a stick. Make 10 the tightest you could imagine, equal to the grip pressure you'd feel if you were hanging on to the still rings like a gymnast. Experiment with what a swing with a grip pressure of 1 feels like. Be prepared to let the club fly out of your hands, but trust me, it won't. Your grip pressure naturally tightens as you approach impact. You should be pleasantly surprised by how much more rhythmic and flowing your swing is at 1 or 2. Most golfers do not know what swings feel like when their grip pressure is too loose. You'll probably find out that what you thought would be way too loose isn't that loose at all.

Do the same with a 10 and see if you sense a difference in your swing. See how easy it is or isn't to hit a big sweeping hook with your hands strangling the grip. Odds are it won't be easy.

Now, starting at 1 on your scale, slowly begin increasing the grip pressure. Ideally, your grip pressure should be between 3 and 5, but under pressure you can easily find it sliding closer to 7, 8, or 9. Knowing what a 1 or a 2 feels like will help you find that ideal low-medium pressure that you need to make the most effective swings. Eventually, you should learn what Tiger Woods learned when he said, "No doubt about it: Light is right."

Problem 2: "Quick" at the Top

Physiologically, fear can make us get "quick" at the top. As with overly tight grip pressure, most of us know this feeling, too. Here, the downswing starts before the club is properly set at the top, so the body begins moving into the shot while the arms are still going back. Why does this happen? Well, tighter muscles and a racing mind are okay if you're trying to execute a relatively one-dimensional task like outracing a saber-toothed tiger before you become his dinner. Tight muscles and a racing mind are not such a good combination if you're trying to execute a relatively unnatural act like hitting a small ball with a small piece of metal and making it go into a small hole far away. Fear can make us want to do things quicker; a properly executed golf swing is controlled, and sometimes that means slower.

words of a champion: payne stewart, 1999 u.s. open

The late Payne Stewart's final victory was unquestionably his most emotional, and in many ways it was his most complete as a supreme champion. Stewart began the final day of the 1999 U.S. Open at Pinehurst's venerable No. 2 course leading by a shot, and in damp, chilly conditions,

cont. on next page

cont. from previous page

refused to buckle under the pressure. He holed out with an iron will, completing the round with only 24 putts, and coming down the stretch, he holed a 25-foot putt at 16, a nervy three-footer for birdie at 17 to retake the lead, and an epic fifteen-footer for par to win his second U.S. Open title. Stewart's assessment in the moments after claiming the trophy reflects a man committed to playing fearless golf: "I wasn't thinking about Phil or Tiger or David or anybody. I was thinking about getting the job done and doing what I had to do to give myself a chance."

Stewart talked about how he had a specific game plan for playing the golf course, hitting certain clubs on particular holes, regardless of the situation. And when it came down to the difficult closing hole, Stewart would not let himself panic even when his tee shot trickled into the rough. Needing a par, he had to trust his game plan and ignore the temptation to try to muscle a long iron from a difficult lie in heavy wet grass. He was left with a fifteen-foot putt, a putt he knew, a putt he had practiced earlier in the week. All that preparation, all that pressure, all that fear and Payne Stewart played fearlessly. "I didn't question how I played the hole," he said in the press tent afterward.

I kind of knew what lie I had, and so I dealt with it. When I got up on the green, I was saying, "Look, you've given yourself a chance. You're here. Do the

cont. on next page

cont. from previous page

same things you've been doing. Believe that you've read it right and make your stroke." So I stood up there and read it. And I said this is an inside left putt, just believe that. And I stood up there and did my routine and kept my head still, and when I looked up it was two feet from the hole and it was breaking right in the center and I couldn't believe it. I couldn't believe that I'd accomplished another dream of mine.

Problem 3: Deceleration

The third way that tension and fear influence the golf swing is that golfers change their rate of acceleration on the downswing. Tennis great Jim Courier once explained to me that when tennis players get nervous they often hit the ball short because they decelerate. The same thing happens to golfers who feel psychological resistance. They decelerate into the ball. On the full swing we call this trying to "steer" the ball or "holding on" too long. When trying to execute chip shots, this deceleration often results in either a thin shot off the blade or a chunked shot where golfers "lay the sod" over it because they swing in a jab motion. When golfers feel fear over a putt, deceleration manifests itself in the form of a "jabbed" putt along with a slight flinch of the eyes and slight movement of the head (which influence direction and line). Why? Well, think about the fight-or-flight syndrome. When you're running from a tiger, you want to know how close he is to biting your leg. So you do what you can to get informed, even looking back over your shoulder when we all know that such a posture isn't the best if you're trying to run your fastest. Well, when you're nervous in golf, your mind is overly occupied with results (not the process), even in the midst of executing a shot. You fear a left shot, so you hold on to the finish. You fear a skulled chip, so you look up and chunk it. Again, the focus is on the result (thanks to the power of fear), when the focus should be on the process.

Problem 4: Coming Out of the Shot

The final way that nervousness translates into the golf swing is that golfers often pull out of shots early. They jerk or flinch and do not stay down through the golf ball. If you are someone who plays a lot of golf, then you are aware that the most common error when golfers lose their confidence and begin playing frightened golf is to block the ball out to the right. Think about it. If you grip the club too tightly, get quick at the top, decelerate into the ball, and then pull out of the shot early, then of course the club face will have the tendency to arrive at the ball in an open position.

Now, how do we go about solving these fear-induced physiological difficulties? Well, there are physical things that you can put into your process of playing golf that may help. First, when it comes to your grip getting too tight, learn to be aware of grip pressure. Let me be clear: The culprit that accounts for the lion's share of those high ballooning blocked shots you see when golfers get nervous is their grip pressure. Most PGA Tour professionals would tell you that, on a scale ranging from 1 (very loose) to 10 (very tight), the ideal grip pressure is between a 3 and a 6. When battling fear, a golfer who usually grips at a 3 will typically grip at a 7 because he is trying to feel the club the way he does when he is confident. However, he will often believe that he is gripping at his normal 3 because that is what registers in his mind. Because we lose feeling in our hands when we are frightened, in the golfer's mind, the only way to feel the club appears to be to grip it more tightly. The result, as I've explained, is to not only get quick at the top but also to interfere with the release of the golf club. Golfers who have too much tension in their hands very often block the ball out to the right because the club does not fully release until it is too late. Once they do release, it is often a quick snap, resulting in just the opposite, the low hook. This is why fear makes cowards of us all in golf. Because you cannot play this game very long if you don't know whether a high fade or a low hook is coming next.

Honestly, it can be as simple as making checking grip pressure a part of your preshot routine. Ben Hogan said that, while he is practicing, he is also cultivating the habit of concentration. Jack Nicklaus suggested that he always practiced how he wanted to play. That said, it is important for golfers to learn their ideal grip pressure. The "swing thought" I give to golfers, which I learned from noted teaching professional Fran Hoxie, is "soft hands," a thought that golfers intuitively understand. During times when pressure overrides thoughts that you cannot control, work to control your grip pressure to ensure proper release of the club. If you're getting too quick, again, the fundamental flaw may lie with grip pressure. If you go to the driving range and experiment with grip pressure, you'll see how difficult it becomes to get quick at the top when one has soft hands. Soft hands, usually the equivalent of a 3 or 4 in grip pressure, often ensure that one sets the club properly at the top.

If fear manifests itself with weak, decelerating, "hold on" type swings, the solution is as simple as training yourself to get to a full finish and then holding that finish position. The golf swing is an emergent, fluid action. Seldom will one thing fix it completely. However, when the mind starts playing tricks on us, it translates into very real, observable, predictable consequences in the golf swing. Our thoughts should always be guided by the question, What is my target? When our body tightens and our mind races, however, as they often will in this game, it takes a little more than a good thought to allow us to hit the ball. If we can soften our grip, accelerate through the ball, and, as Butch Harmon likes to say, "shake hands with the target," then we are by default trusting our swing and giving ourselves a better chance to play fearless golf.

But as crucial as these physical efforts to fight our fears might be, the vital and much more fundamental area of our games that we need to attack is the entire mental approach.

Fixing the physical flaws requires time on the range, building a repeatable swing you can trust. Fixing the mental approach requires something more. It gets right to the heart of the essential question that got us here in the first place: Why do you play golf?

CHAPTER 2

Mastery and Ego in Golf

Sometimes superstardom is a given, but when it is announced on an overcast day in the Pacific Northwest in late August with all of golf watching with bated breath, it quickly turns fact into phenomenon. We should have known Tiger Woods's performance on the final day of the U.S. Amateur in 1996 was coming; history had shown us glimpses in the past. He once won a U.S. Junior after being two down with two holes to play. He won his first NCAA title despite shooting an 80. He won his first U.S. Amateur title by rallying from five down with thirteen to play. In short, even at the most extreme of circumstances, his confidence always appeared to be unfazed.

But nothing could compare or prepare us for Woods on his final day as an amateur amid the lush green and towering pines of Pumpkin Ridge Golf Club and the 1996 U.S.

Amateur Championship. Facing an inspired though relatively unknown Steve Scott in the 36-hole final, Woods somehow rallied from being five down after the morning eighteen. Repeatedly, Scott was able to answer the charging Woods, who cut the deficit to 1-down twice only to see Scott push it back. It was grand theater before a swelling crowd of some 19,000 following the lone two-ball on the course all day, and the roars of the players and fans took on the scope of two warriors clashing in the Colosseum. On the final day, Woods hit 28 of the last 29 greens in regulation, shot a 65 for the final 18 holes, and rolled in circus-like putts of forty-five feet for eagle and thirty-five feet for birdie on the back nine.

When he won on the thirty-eighth hole, his exchange with reporters after hoisting the trophy seemed almost unbelievably matter of fact, but it clearly showed the sort of grace under fire that the great ones develop.

Q: Going out, you're five down going to the first tee in the afternoon. What are your thoughts?

TIGER WOODS: I was feeling very confident.

Q: Really?

TIGER WOODS: Yeah. I worked some stuff out with Butch on the range. Worked on my putting and got back in the groove again, and felt very confident going out. One, it's in the past. It's over and done with. I've been there before. Instead of being five down with 13 to play, I'm five down and 18. It was a comfortable feeling.

Q: In the tighter matches, you seem to put yourself in a frame of mind that allows you to focus and slow everything down.

TIGER WOODS: All I do is stay in my same routine. Even though I have certain putts that are bigger than others, you never see me out of rhythm, I always stay the same pace, do everything the same. So what I did the first hole today and the last hole today is exactly the same. There's no change. I think that's probably one of the biggest keys. That's what Nicklaus was so good at. You could time him. Every routine he had was exactly the same.

As seen this day in Oregon and proven time after time in the years that would follow, Tiger is as great a winner as the game of golf has ever known. Greatness such as this prevails not merely because it is great, but because it knows what to do to make it possible to be great—and then it does not waver from that path, regardless of the circumstances.

Tiger epitomizes the fearless golfer. Certainly, his style of play can be heroic and exciting, but it is his steely resolve in the most pressured situations that makes him a compelling case study. It is no secret that Woods has taken many of the cues for his career from the attitude and the achievements of Jack Nicklaus. From his youngest days, Jack Nicklaus was well known for his attention to the details of *two things*: the mechanics of his golf swing and the most minute distinctions of each golf course. Jack carefully measured distances of the courses on which he played. He studied them closely and meticulously. He never misunderstood the unalterable truth that golf is always a game between just two players: a golfer and the golf course on which he is playing. Nicklaus once was asked his earliest memories of Pebble Beach, which he first saw when he went there in 1961 to play—and win—the U.S. Amateur. He answered,

> I saw the course at Pebble Beach and I thought the same things I thought about Augusta National. I liked walking down Magnolia Lane, but I really wanted to play the course itself. I'd heard all about the tradition, but for me I really just wanted to play the course, learn about it, and test it out.

Jack was not interested in the rumor mill, predictions about who would win, or the personal affairs of other golfers. He was not really caught up in the people, prestige, or history of tournaments called The Masters, the U.S. Open, and the U.S. Amateur. His mind was squarely focused on the grass fairways, greens, and conditions of golf courses called Augusta National and Pebble Beach. That is mastery golf epitomized. Mastery golf, as you will find below, is the beginning of the path to fearless golf.

jonathan byrd on a lifelong focus

Second-year PGA Tour player and 2002 Rookie of the Year Jonathan Byrd highlights the upcoming class of "young

cont. on next page

cont. from previous page

guns" with his mastery approach to the game. Despite struggling with injury and recovering from surgery in 2003 and early 2004, Byrd put himself in contention in the middle of 2004. His solid focus led to consistent shot-making down the stretch of the B.C. Open and a one-stroke victory. An excerpt from one of our recent conversations shows that Jonathan—much like his hero Ben Hogan—is the classic profile of a mastery golfer in the making.

BYRD: I think in middle school and high school I liked a lot of different sports but golf was something I latched on to. I liked practicing by myself. I didn't mind after school just going until dark and practicing. It was just something I liked to do and that is the biggest reason . . . it is cliché I guess . . . but love of the game. I love to practice. I love to get better. And ever since second grade the process of learning new shots, or learning how to hit flop shots, or just learning how to do something technically better is the biggest reason I like to play golf. Just getting better in all aspects of the game is so fun.

DR. VALIANTE: Hogan said tournaments were anticlimactic to practice.

BYRD: I agree. I like the work better. I think the work is the most satisfying. Like last year, winning that golf tour-

cont. on next page

cont. from previous page

nament was like icing on the cake. But I didn't need it. I didn't need to win to know that I was getting better. I could see it and feel it in my practice.

VALIANTE: What is it about that process you like so much?

BYRD: You're just perfecting something. You are never going to perfect it but you are getting closer to it. You are learning. You are getting better. You're learning new shots. Your swing is getting technically better and just getting really good at something is really satisfying regardless of who I beat or where I finish.

Becoming better at anything, whether it's golf or business or teaching or rocket science, always begins with asking the right questions. Let me then ask you a simple question: Why do you play golf? Take a moment to write down what you believe are the primary reasons why you play golf. Be sure to list them in order of importance. Believe it or not, understanding the implications behind the answer to this simple question can help you improve your golf game more than additional lessons or new clubs.

Looking at your list, the reasons you came up with are probably similar to the reasons provided by most golfers. If you are a professional or aim to be one, you love the game and enjoy the competition, and you enjoy the feeling of knowing you're so good at something, perhaps even better than most others. You love to win. If you're a professional golfer, chances are that your underlying motives for playing with members of your own family are not the same as those for competing against your friends or competing in an important tournament.

the search for *kaizen*

In business, there is a fascination these days with the Japanese word "*kaizen*." It is used in business terms to apply to the idea of an intense effort to improve a process or system by eliminating all nonessential elements as waste. Directly translated from the Japanese, *kaizen* is a simpler concept but more vital to the development of the fearless golfer. Specifically, *kaizen* is the idea of continual, measured improvement, regardless of performance. That last phrase is essential. This is what defines a mastery golfer. The mastery golfer is not discouraged by an initial lack of success, rather he is excited at the prospect of the challenge. Mastery golfers who demonstrate *kaizen* get lost in the details, puzzles, and mysteries of the game, and they see their task as mastering those details and understanding the game's mysteries. In *kaizen*, you embrace the process on your own terms and you are totally in control of your own improvement. In *kaizen*, the game lies subservient to your process of improvement. Improvement is a constant goal, yet it happens not simply because it is a goal, but because the focus on the process allows it to happen.

If you golf for recreation, no doubt you love the game as well, and perhaps you enjoy competing against your buddies. It's likely that you find golf a great way to relax and recharge the batteries. If you're a recreational golfer, you likely have reasons for playing in the annual company outing or the club championship that are unrelated to playing a leisurely round with your friends.

In professional psychology, the reasons why individuals choose to engage in a particular task or activity are called *achievement goal orientations*. That's fancy language, but what it means essentially is that we choose to do something for a certain end, a particular objective; in short, we are motivated by the activity because in some way it enhances our sense of self, our personal well-being. Those objectives govern our approach to the activity from the outset. These orientations are critical factors that influence a person's level of motivation and achievement, as well as the degree of anxiety and fear they experience as they engage in those activities.

ben hogan's real secret

Ben Hogan won sixty-four times in his professional career, nine of them major championships. Fifty of those wins, including all of the majors, came after his thirty-third birthday. While many observers of the game suggest that

cont. on next page

cont. from previous page

Hogan's improved mechanics were the source of his success, Hogan himself believed at least a little bit that there was more to it than the famous Five Fundamentals he and author Herbert Warren Wind wrote about in their famous instruction book. Certainly, Hogan was relentless in his pursuit of perfecting his golf swing. That's the *kaizen* we've talked about before. That attention to constant improvement led some to suggest that Hogan had unearthed some sort of secret to the technique of the golf swing. Because Hogan never really answered questions about what his secret might be, books and magazines in the years since have often tried to discover what this minuscule bit of mechanics was. Maybe there was something Hogan did with his left wrist or right forefinger that keyed his repeatable swing, but what keyed his success in the game may not have been totally physical. Indeed, Hogan suggests it went beyond the mere execution of the golf swing. Hogan relentlessly focused on the task at hand. His mind was constantly occupied with the variables that might influence the next golf shot. In other words, his battles were always personal, always between himself and the golf course. Ben Hogan's real secret? Concentration. "I didn't win in the 1930s because I hadn't yet learned to concentrate," he once wrote, "to ignore the gallery and the other golfers, and to shut my mind against everything but my own game." Have you learned to narrow your focus and to shut your mind? You don't have to be Ben Hogan to learn that kind of skill.

The primary motivation for some golfers, whether they are average golfers or tour players, is to earn recognition from others. For these golfers, what others say about them is powerfully important, sometimes more important than improving and developing their game. While preparing to hit an important shot, their minds are often divided: One side of their mind is trying to focus on executing the golf shot, but the other side is busy worrying about what other people will think if they blow the shot. One can easily understand how such extraneous concerns can interfere with the mechanics of golf. Rather than being lost in the thought of hitting the precise shot they want, golfers whose attention is focused on raising their personal stock in the eyes of others often become indecisive and uncertain with the club in their hands. These motivations, these emotions are not necessarily at the forefront of our thinking, but they lurk in the shadows, and their presence can be a subtle but powerful influence. Of course, as all golfers know, the quickest way to unravel a golf swing is to introduce any type of uncertainty and indecision into one's mind. It doesn't matter if you're a professional golfer who is preoccupied with the fear of his scores being posted in the paper the next day, or the rank beginner who's afraid others will think less of him if he doesn't hit a good shot. In either case, the focus of their attention is misplaced.

The golfer who thinks this way exhibits what psychologists call an ego orientation.

In contrast to those who play because they want the attention and admiration of others, some golfers have as their primary incentive a desire to learn, improve, and excel. A focus on learning and personal development is inconsistent with worries about how our results will be viewed by others. Professional golfers who play to excel are better able to disregard outside contingencies like rankings, scores, other peoples' opinions, and even prize money. A recreational golfer whose reason for playing is to learn and grow, and even relax, cares very little about how others in his foursome will view his drive. In both of these cases, a golfer's attention is on things related to hitting better golf shots: swing mechanics, strategy, course conditions, thickness of the rough, tempo, and location of hazards. Because their minds are undivided as they prepare to hit a golf shot (rather than being disrupted by the potential reactions to the golf shot), these golfers are better able to stay focused and remain composed during their round. And rest assured that they're enjoying themselves a good deal more and worrying a lot less than their self-obsessed and self-conscious counterparts.

mastery drill no. 1: focus on the golf course

Recall that among Jack Nicklaus's great traits as the premier mastery golfer was his relentless focus on the golf course as his primary opponent. Nicklaus was so intent on studying the course that he became relatively oblivious to everything else around him.

cont. on next page

cont. from previous page

You can't teach that tremendous concentration, but even the average golfer can set himself up for developing that kind of focus. It's what I like to think of as a distraction with a purpose. For your next round of golf, instead of showing up, grabbing a scorecard, and heading to the first tee, make a concerted effort to study the course hole-by-hole. If you have time, attempt to plan out the round shot by shot, deciding which par 4s absolutely require a driver, where the safe misses are on par 3s and whether there's a par 5 you can attack. Don't purchase a yardage book as a souvenir, use it like you would a good caddie, consulting it on every tee box.

The key with such a distraction is that it forces you to focus on the golf course. Often when I chat with a player before a tournament, I like to make sure he has spent some time studying the course and its architect and other information about the design. I often am armed with tidbits of knowledge so I can pass that along ahead of time. That way the player will be reminded of the golf course during the round rather than thinking of his score, his standing on the money list, or the status of other players. Whatever your ability level and whatever the circumstances of your round, your attention should be just as singly devoted as a tour player's. And the first step toward developing that focus is to immerse yourself in knowledge about the course and its individual holes and in developing a strategy to play it.

If you recognize yourself in these different reasons for playing golf, don't be surprised. Such orientations are common in many professional endeavors. Public speaking often fills people with the same type of fear as golf. Even in this most dreaded of activities, people whose reason for speaking is to present information and enjoy themselves typically fare better than people whose reason for speaking is to have the audience perceive them as smart or to avoid looking like a babbling idiot. Musicians who strive to perfect a piece of music perform with greater passion and fluidity than do musicians who crave audience approval and fear being booed off the stage.

The key distinction I am drawing can be thought of as the difference between striving to perfect one's task versus striving to look good in front of others or fearing their disapproval. This is a distinction that many golfers know very well.

words of a champion: davis love iii, 2003 at&t pebble beach pro-am

Davis went into Sunday with the lead, but was overtaken by Tom Lehman who shot a front nine 30. In the last group standing on the eighteenth tee, Davis needed par to tie, birdie to win. With water running down the left fairway of the par 5, Davis ripped a 315-yard drive down the middle

cont. on next page

cont. from previous page
and then hit a 4-iron onto the green for a two-putt birdie. How was he able to hit such great shots in such a demanding situation? The answer is that he wasn't playing the situation. He was playing the shot, and thinking about a target.

> I saw what Tom [Lehman] was doing, sure. And I was nervous. But when I was on the 18th tee I was focused on the point on the skylight on the tent on the right side of the fairway. That was my target. I was trying my hardest to focus on the target, not the situation. And after that, once I had my target, just trying to make a fearless swing.

Standing on the tee box, the situation tried to force Davis's mind into bad, ego-oriented questions about the situation such as, Why am I nervous? What if I hit into the water? What if I lose the tournament? However, his discipline, training, and experience allowed him to shrug off those negative thoughts and focus on a target. He decided instead to focus his mind on a target that, at that point, was the top of a sponsor's tent in the distance. Asking himself, What is my target?, Davis then made a fearless golf swing at his target resulting in a perfect drive that he followed up with a perfect second shot into the par 5 for a two-putt birdie, and his first professional win in three years.

Everyone has heard about the "back of the mind." Golfers often say things like, "I was trying to concentrate on making the putt, but in the back of my mind I was thinking 'Don't push it.' " The achievement orientations that I discuss in this chapter often constitute those things that creep into the back of a golfer's mind. So, if you are one of those golfers who has distracting thoughts that lead to hesitation or apprehension, read closely. Identify your own achievement orientations and you can unravel a significant part of the psychological mystery that plagues many golfers who come undone on the course.

Let's have a close look at this psychological process that psychologists consider critical to human motivation. Achievement goal orientations—the underlying reasons why golfers play golf—can be separated into two main categories: mastery orientation and ego orientation. Only one of these approaches will work regardless of the circumstances, only one will work for any golfer regardless of ability, only one will make it possible to play fearless golf.

mastery golf

Golf to me is a livelihood in doing the thing that I love to do. I don't like the glamour. I just like the game.

—BEN HOGAN

People who have a mastery orientation toward an activity engage in that activity because they want to continually learn, refine, and master it regardless of their level of expertise. Guided by the constant striving to improve their skills and do things better each time, mastery-oriented people are driven to elevate their abilities to new levels. In the world of golf, this means that golfers approach the game as a challenge that allows for the sustained refinement of skills.

words of a champion: tiger woods, 2000 u.s. open

Tiger Woods's career of incredible accomplishments may be forever unmatched by his 15-stroke victory in the 2000 U.S. Open at Pebble Beach. Woods finished at an unheard of score of 12 under par at a championship where a score of even par is usually the goal of the championship committee. Woods began the final day with the trophy well in hand, leading by ten shots. He could have played the final round with a lack of focus or intensity, but that is not how Tiger Woods plays the game. He played the final round without making a bogey, including a gritty fifteen-footer for par at the sixteenth hole that on the surface was relatively meaningless. But that's the focus of a man playing fearless golf. His comments to the media reveal the focus of a champion:

cont. on next page

cont. from previous page

I told Stevie [Williams, Tiger's caddie] walking up 18, there comes a point in time when you feel tranquil, when you feel calm. You feel at ease with yourself. For some reason, things just flowed. And no matter what you do, good or bad, it really doesn't get to you. Even the days when you wake up on the wrong side of the bed, for some reason, it doesn't feel too bad; it's just all right.

That feeling comes with confidence, of course, a true sense of self-efficacy that is unwavering and consistent, whether you're on the practice range or eighteenth tee.

"I've always had a tremendous belief in my abilities," Woods said at Pebble Beach. "I've proven it in tournaments, but more so, I've proven it in practice sessions when no one's been around. As a kid pretending to play against some of the best players, trying to imitate their golf swings. And those are the times that you've proved to yourself you can do it. Then you go ahead and do it in competition, and then it feeds from there."

For example, hall-of-famer Nick Price has won forty tournaments in his career on five continents, he has won three major titles and been ranked number one in the world. Now, in his late forties, he still is striving to make his golf swing better.

Part of the reason I have been able to compete for so long is because every year I have refined my golf swing. I have all the same moves I had when I was 19 years old but every year I have just refined it. I have worked diligently to improve my swing that little fraction more because the fact is, it is imperfectible. To me the swing is like a square block of wood, and your goal is to shape that block into the most perfect circle you can. You can get it to a circle pretty quickly, but after you get the general shape right, you then have to refine constantly and perpetually, and go from a hammer and a chisel, to 50 grit sandpaper, to 100 grit sandpaper, to 1000 grit sandpaper, to steel wool, to polish. And every year you refine, regardless of how good your previous year was, you try to get better. And that is what I have tried to do. Better and better every year regardless of where I am. Excellence, it's like a process, you know? No matter where you are, you just keep trying to refine.

Mastery golfers who demonstrate *kaizen* get lost in the details, puzzles, and mysteries of the game, and they see their task as mastering those details and understanding the game's mysteries. Because they view mastering golf as a constant challenge, they find it easy to become fully involved in what they are doing, whether practicing chip shots or putting in competition. Their motivation for playing golf is not prize money, not trophies, not awards, and not accolades or approval from others. For mastery-oriented golfers, the shot matters much more than its consequences. Awards, trophies, and public recognition are seen as natural consequences to excellence, not the primary motive for achieving that excellence.

david duval: mastery orientation

David Duval is one of the most remarkable athletes I've ever met, both for the abundance of his talent and the strength of his character. He eloquently spoke about the competing orientations that arise from being a private individual on a public stage. Here is a portion of one of our talks.

DR. VALIANTE: When you're playing competitive golf, against whom are you competing? The course, other players, a score, yourself?

DAVID DUVAL: Typically you're fighting yourself. You can say you're playing the field or the golf course, or the situation. But truth is you're playing yourself, and that's really how it goes. You're just competing against yourself.

DR. VALIANTE: What part of yourself?

DAVID DUVAL: I think what you're competing against is the part of you that wants to see how you're doing com-

cont. on next page

cont. from previous page

pared to others, wants to see how you're doing in relation to par, wants to analyze whether you're hitting
fairways and greens and making birdies. It goes to
scoreboard watching sometimes. When all is right,
when your head is right, it is easy to remember that
golf is a series of eighteen scores that you add up
when you're done. That it is an accumulation of shots.
There's really no excuse not to do that, but that's not
always the easiest thing to do. So you're competing
against yourself. You should be executing what you're
trying to do relative to the golf course and your game.

Mastery golfers enjoy everything that golf throws at them.
The greater the challenge, the more fun they have. For them,
the golf swing becomes an automatic process. Because they
focus on improvement relative to their own current capabilities, their standards and goals are self-set rather than set by
others. Mastery golfers do not care who their competitors are,
because they don't view golf as a competition between players. Rather, they see golf as the process of playing a golf course
as well as they can with the skills that they possess. They
know that golf is at times unpredictable, and, although they
cannot control the unpredictable, they react the same way
each time: with increased effort, determination, and passion
for playing. Mastery golfers are neither swayed by praise nor
bothered by criticism. They know full well that approval is

fleeting and people are fickle. Those who raved about you on Saturday may come to possess such high expectations that they will be disapproving on Sunday. And so, mastery golfers are not influenced by how often others tell them they are good or they are bad because, quite frankly, they do not play for others. They play to achieve goals they have set for themselves, and they use only those self-set standards to measure their improvement. Mastery golfers care about their games, and not about what others have to say about their games. They are their own fan club and their own best critic, and they play golf with a quiet mind, focusing only on the things within their control. For mastery golfers, playing golf—whether in a tournament, competition, weekend outing, company event, or family get-together—is not a means to an end. Playing golf is an end in itself.

mastery drill: the default answer

As we've said, mastery golfers are complex thinkers with a simple focus. One key to developing a simple focus is to stubbornly refuse to let yourself think about anything circumstantial. Ultimately, there is no benefit to scoreboard watching because scoreboard watching often serves no purpose other than to distract us from the singular, target-oriented process that breeds success.

cont. on next page

cont. from previous page

Therefore, the mastery golfer should be able to answer any dilemma, any difficult situation, with a three-word answer. Shout it, tattoo it to your forearm, but remember it: *What's my target?*

Here's a drill: As you play a practice round, have a friend periodically ask you what you are thinking. That question all by itself should immediately prompt you to ask yourself, "What's my target?"

Consider the following scenarios. As varied and complex as they are, each has the same answer.

If you birdie the first three holes, what do you ask yourself on the fourth tee?

A. What's my target?

If you shoot 42 on the front nine and are trying to break 90 for the first time, what do you ask yourself on the tenth tee?

A. What's my target?

If you've bogeyed the first three holes on the back nine and then double-bogeyed the next three, what are you thinking on the sixteenth tee?

A. What's my target?

It is easy to understand how to apply the ideal mastery orientation to tournament golf. But what of those of us who will never play tournaments? Does mastery golf have an application? Certainly it does. In fact, it makes fundamental improvement possible regardless of the skill level. A mastery approach does not necessarily require a focus on shooting a particular score at the start of the day; instead it requires an exacting focus on hitting a particular shot with a particular routine at a particular target as often as it takes to hole out eighteen times.

herman edwards and the power of honesty

As we've discussed, perhaps fear's most sinister quality is that it can be largely irrational. It overtakes us because we lose the ability to logically focus on the object of the game. We worry about a hundred different things, except for the principal challenge of the exercise. Sometimes we forget that the object of the game of golf is not to make pretty swings or even to hit fairways and greens. The object of the game is to get the ball in the hole. That sort of frankness gets lost in the minor hysteria that can freeze a system that operates in fear, what Johnny Miller has sometimes referred to as Stage 3 Choking.

When I think about this sort of situation, I'm reminded of what football coach Herman Edwards once said to a less than clear-thinking member of the New York media after his Jets had gotten off to a 2 and 5 start. With the team on the verge of being eliminated from playoff contention, the reporter wondered if his team might be giving up. Edwards was frustrated and tense, but he hadn't lost focus. He also experienced the restorative power of a simple,

cont. on next page

cont. from previous page

undeniable truth. How Edwards responded to the question
of whether his team was on the verge of quitting motivated
his players to a strong finish and an unexpected AFC East
championship.

> Oh, no, they're not going to do that, no. It's inex-
> cusable. It's called being a professional. That's
> part of the deal. If they're going to do that—that's
> players, coaches, management, anybody—then
> they need to go somewhere else.
>
> See, the problem is, this is what happens when
> you lose. People start assuming they quit. Well,
> this team ain't doing that. It's not an option.
> Retirement, yeah. Quitting, no. You don't do that
> in sports. It's ridiculous. That's crazy.
>
> This is what the greatest thing about sports is:
> You play to win the game. HELLO?! You play to win
> the game.

Next time bad results leave you discouraged, remember the simple message of a direct answer to a direct question: Why do you play? You play to win the game. So go out
and do everything you can to win it, whether "winning" for
you means claiming your first U.S. Open or parring the last
two holes to break 90.

hogan, nicklaus, and woods: models of mastery golf

That which connects Ben Hogan, Jack Nicklaus, and Tiger Woods across time is more than the fact that each dominated their generation in the game of golf. Almost in a connect-the-dots manner, each man's approach to the game was pointedly similar. So much so, in fact, that it is difficult to see where Hogan's hawklike gaze ends and Nicklaus's intense stare begins; where Jack's wholehearted consumption with the game ends and Tiger's unflinching dedication to the sport begins.

Nicklaus's teacher, Jack Grout, was the assistant pro where young Ben Hogan caddied. Hogan and Grout played the Tour together and, when he inherited the young Nicklaus as a student, Grout often used "Bennie" Hogan as the model toward which Nicklaus should strive. Similarly, Tiger Woods was in awe of Nicklaus (he grew up with a poster of Jack on his wall) and patterned his own career after Jack's. A study of the three men is like watching waves in the ocean—impossible to isolate where one wave ends and the next begins. Regardless of similarities and differences in practice habits and swing mechanics, their mental approach to the game is unmistakably mastery oriented. They are not only master golfers, but mastery golfers. In fact, they are master golfers *because* they are mastery golfers.

Here is a great illustration of this point. Back problems al-

most prevented Jack Nicklaus from competing in the 2002
Memorial Tournament. A friend urged Jack to play because it
would give the fans a thrill. Jack's reply suggested a unique
bond between the legend he imitated (Hogan), and the legend
who imitates him (Tiger). Jack said,

> I don't want to go out there, shoot 85, and wave to every-
> body with a false smile on my face. That's not me. I've got
> to be able to play because I get my enjoyment from play-
> ing golf, not waving. People are great, but I can't go out
> and play for them. I've got to play for me. That's the only
> way I can play. If I play for me and I do well for me, then
> I'll do well for them. And certainly that's what I've always
> done. Now maybe that's selfish. I don't know. But it's the
> way that I think if you're going to be a golfer, you got to
> play golf. You've got to do that. That's the way I played
> all my life. I think Tiger plays that way. He has to play
> Tiger's game and do what he does. That's how Hogan
> played as well.

Compare that with what Jonathan Byrd said about his reasons for playing.

> When it is all said and done, it is more fun the hours I've
> had practicing until dark when it is just me and my in-
> structor and the game. It is just so much more satisfying.
> Those times are much funner than standing in front of a

crowd and them all seeing you and cheering you on . . . that's great too, but the hours working on it when nobody is there is more satisfying. I hope to always stay that way—you never know if you will because money and stuff changes people—but I don't think I will ever not enjoy that. Part of it is that purity. You know I can't say—I mean I love to compete and winning is a lot—but I enjoy the process of making my swing more perfect, purer, shots more pure . . . everything from the sound, the speed, the club how it hits the turf is so exciting. It is not just get the ball from point A to point B . . . it is more about making it all purer and more perfect.

Because mastery golfers play the game for the personal challenge it provides rather than for the recognition they receive from others, their concentration is invariably on the golf course and not on the other golfers, the gallery, the scoreboard, or even on their own score. While watching his pursuers falter on Sunday as Tiger won the 2002 Masters, Jack Nicklaus insightfully observed,

They [other golfers] were playing Tiger when they should have played the golf course. I think it was quite obvious that they were trying to do things that they shouldn't be trying to do. And they found themselves all of a sudden trying to do things, instead of playing the course and playing their game, they're looking at a leaderboard trying to play somebody else. Tiger played his own game. And that's the way you play this game. You play the golf course. You play the game.

Ben Hogan's name has become synonymous with excellence, dedication, and concentration. The man they called "the Hawk" relentlessly focused on the task of zeroing in on a completely flawlessly reliable swing. Among the more memorable quips attributed to him over the years was his assessment that "there are not enough hours in the day to practice all the shots you need to be great," and "any day spent not practicing . . ." His mind was constantly occupied with the variables that might influence the golf shot. In other words, his battles were always personal, always between himself and the course or himself and the swing.

Why is a mastery approach so critical to ultimately being able to play fearless golf? Well, in a large way, that's what this book is about. But to understand it simply, think of the task of playing your best golf as you would having to make a 500-mile car trip. If you were to focus on the monotony or the ten hours of traffic jams or the simple inconvenience of driving 500 miles, the enormity of it might prevent you from getting in the car in the first place. But if you focused instead on the act of driving one mile 500 times, the task doesn't seem so overwhelming, or seems at least a little more doable. The key is to let your mind get lost in the process. To reverse an old parable, to play fearless golf you have to focus on the trees and lose sight of the forest. The mastery golfer gets consumed with the task of executing shots, not with the prospect of breaking 90 or shooting 65. The score is merely an aftereffect of an attention to the details of playing the golf course.

mickelson and mastery vs. ego

Phil Mickelson is widely acknowledged as one of the most talented golfers in golf. But prior to his Masters victory in 2004, he had routinely been characterized as a player who could not rally at the truly big moments. Phil's remarks from his performance at the 2002 U.S. Open at Bethpage Black suggest that he sometimes falls into the category of a golfer who plays with an eye to beating other players, shooting scores, and where he stands in relation to the field. Because he is so talented, this mindset works well enough to have won him twenty tournaments, and a lifetime exemption on Tour. Nonetheless, is it ideal?

Before the 2001 Masters, Phil said he would like to win the Masters in order to "become part of the history of the game." This is a mindset that is ego-oriented and outcome focused rather than mastery and process focused. However, once he abandons that thinking and focuses on himself and the course, things sometimes change. At the 2002 U.S. Open he shot scores of 70, 73, 67, 70. His best round of 67 came only after he thought he'd shot himself out of the tournament, at which point here's what

cont. on next page

cont. from previous page
he said (the emphasis is mine, but the intent of his words
is clear):

> The last thing on my mind was trying to get in con-
> tention to win this tournament because even if I
> get it back, if Tiger goes out and shoots three or
> four under par, it wouldn't make any difference.
> But I was able to not worry about what the leaders
> were doing, and try to get my round back to even
> par. Just play the golf course.

ego golf

In contrast to mastery golfers, ego golfers are primarily guided
by their desire either to appear competent in front of other
people or to avoid looking incompetent. The defining features
of golfers who possess an ego orientation include a concern
with appearing capable, demonstrating superior ability relative to others, and being motivated to play well to show off for
others. But there is another, more insidious, side to an ego orientation. The driving force of many ego golfers is not simply
to demonstrate their ability and receive the approval of others,
but to avoid at all costs being embarrassed by a poor performance. Such golfers live in very real fear of the embarrassment
they may suffer at almost any moment. Ego golfers put a great

deal of stock on matters that are only distantly and superficially related to actually playing golf. For them, a round of golf is closely aligned with the mindset people adopt for "image management." Golf is merely a means to the end of boosting their ego, status, and reputation. Of course, as you will come to understand, it is a pretty suspect support system. It is their chance to shine. It's not about golf (the task), it's about them (and their ego).

When ego golfers are playing with confidence, they have their ego-boosting goals in sight and they see those goals as achievable. They are playing well, swinging with authority, and are getting the recognition that feeds them. All eyes are on them, and all hearts are at their feet. At times like this, ego golfers know that the way they are playing will lead to what they want from golf: prestige, stature, attention from friends or fans, money, awards, the boss's approving nods. Their ears are pinned back, their egos are being fed, and they are leaning into every shot. The fact, however, is that they have something to prove.

When things go well for the ego-oriented golfer, it is not difficult to understand how they could well feel a sense of euphoria. Showing off feels really good, and recognition is a wonderful aphrodisiac. Who doesn't want to feel this way? But the approval of others rests on very shaky ground, and playing for others has its own set of consequences. Golfers who play to bolster their ego will indeed have their ego bolstered—but only if they are successful. As the saying goes, success is a cheating spouse, especially in a fickle and fluctuating game like golf.

The Story of Mike: A Rising Star

Mike was a twenty-two-year-old golfer who had come to see me in the summer of 1999. Mike had been an excellent junior player who had finished well at several AJGA (American Junior Golf Association) tournaments. He'd won his club championship by a record number, and after an excellent junior year in high school, Mike was ranked by several national publications as one of the best high school golfers in the nation. In the small, elite world of competitive golf, Mike was beginning to turn heads. His parents beamed at his achievements, and in the small town in Georgia where he was from, he was even treated as something of a celebrity.

When he practiced at the club, members would stop and watch in awe. At the snack bar inside the clubhouse, he heard people whisper his name. "Isn't that the kid who shot 4-under in the club championship?" He was accurate with his irons. He was long off the tee. And he had an incredible touch around the greens. The questions surrounding Mike were not "whether" he would be on the PGA Tour, but "when" he would be on the PGA Tour. We all have our own "personal fables"—imaginary narratives that we use to describe our lives—and in Mike's fable, he was a shining star on the rise.

The messages from the outside world seeped into Mike's head, and the praise and attention were, to him, nothing short of intoxicating. He began to relish the attention and status that came with being such a good golfer. He liked to read his name in print, to hear his name whispered, to be respected for his game, and to be feared in competition.

During the summer before he was to attend college, something happened that would have a dramatic effect on Mike. One morning, while jogging along the road, Mike tripped over a stone, fell to the pavement, and broke his wrist. The nature of the break was serious and would require several delicate surgeries. The prognosis was that the wrist would be in a cast for at least four months, and it would be at least a year and a half before it could withstand the torment of serious practice. In the millisecond it takes for a delicate wrist bone to crack, Mike's life had changed.

It is said that time heals all things. In this case, that cliché was only partly true. Time did heal Mike's body. But just as time healed the body, it had a funny way of playing tricks with the mind. The world of golf did not stop and wait for Mike's wrist to heal. It went on without him, and as other golfers began to steal the spotlight and attention, Mike felt left behind. Not to play, not to compete, and to feel that he didn't belong disturbed Mike greatly. His commitment to return to competitive golf was passionate and intense, and he literally launched himself into rehabilitation and exercise.

Six months out of his last cast, and two full years after the accident, Mike finally found himself once again leading a golf tournament. But though he had prepared for the *physical* challenges of tournament golf, he found himself facing something for which he had *not* prepared. For the first time in his life, Mike felt *anxious* on the golf course. Standing on the tenth tee, he got a sinking feeling in his stomach, his mind was overcome by dreadful thoughts, his body tightened, his hands shook, and he ended up shooting 79 on a day when the scores were generally low. He'd lost by five strokes in front of a hometown crowd to players he used to beat routinely. He felt humiliated and foolish. "Like a choking dog," he said. From that day forward, Mike was unable to play well. Competition sent him into a panic, and instead of looking forward to tournaments, he dreaded them. His approach to golf was total ego avoid. That was when, at the recommendation of a mutual friend, he came to visit me.

As I spent more time with Mike and I came to better understand his story, it became clear that as a youngster, Mike had taken a mastery approach to the game of golf (as most children do). He practiced and played whenever he could. He had unbridled enthusiasm for learning and improvement. After school he would ride his bike to the club and hit balls until it was dark. In the summertime he would arrive early in the morning, and he would play golf all day until the late summer sun would set and cast tall shadows across the greens. He loved to practice and he loved to play. He would try out new shots, invent games for himself, and get lost in hours of experimentation and mastery. Growing up, the reward for playing golf was playing golf. His motivation was learning and improvement, and he was never satisfied. He had *kaizen* built into his bones. If he had improved at something from one day to the next, he was happy that he was moving in the right direction. If he got stuck on specific skills, he didn't get mad, he got curious. So he would visit the pro and ask question after question. And when he first began to enter competitions, he did so for the love of the game. The excitement of competing in junior events was playing a new course, meeting new players, and testing his skills to hit different shots. His satisfaction was measured against the goals that he had set for himself. If he could do something better today than he did yesterday, he felt like he was growing. And so he was happy.

As you can imagine, such unbridled enthusiasm for learning and improvement, coupled with a good degree of natural talent, made Mike a pretty good golfer. He entered the junior club championship and won. People applauded. His parents took his picture. He entered the regular club championship and won. More people applauded. Newspapers took his picture. He entered the state Junior Open and won. Galleries applauded. Magazines took his picture. The newspaper put his face on the sports page with the heading "Hometown Hero." In town and at the club people would ask his parents about him and his golf game. Without even being aware of what was happening, Mike was beginning to relish the attention that golf brought him. It wasn't long before the first thing that he would do after executing a great golf shot was look around to see who was watching. If no one saw it, he was disappointed. After good rounds he would quickly head into the clubhouse for a soda, waiting for someone to ask how he played. He would talk endlessly after good rounds of golf, and be silent after poor rounds.

Competitive golf outside the club also began to take on a new meaning. The amount of preparation he did for a tournament was directly correlated to the prestige of the tournament. How excited he got depended on the attention that the tournament got. More prestigious tournaments got more practice time, and he paid more attention to detail. He looked forward to tournaments as much for the opportunity to give an interview as for the chance to play a new golf course. He also gave more effort for bigger tournaments and got more upset if he didn't perform well in them. In short, Mike got caught in a cycle of detrimental ego-oriented thinking that was triggered by everything around him. As his achievement orientation strengthened, the admiration of the golf community took precedence (a community that pays attention to wins, losses, rankings, and scores). Because he was so talented, and on full ego-approach mode, Mike was able to perform at high levels. He felt invincible.

The accident changed all that. On returning to golf, Mike was no longer the center of everyone's attention. People no longer watched him practice, and not many people saw him as a threat in tournaments. He was rarely interviewed.

As I mentioned, Mike had a powerful desire to make a comeback, but in thinking back on that time, Mike realized that his comeback was fueled by his desire to prove himself to others, to regain the spotlight, and to show everyone that he was a great golfer. Mike had fantasies of stunning the golf world, of the interviews he would give detailing his comeback, and of accepting trophies.

All the work he had done—the running, the lifting weights, and rehabilitation—was connected in his mind to an extremely dominant ego mentality. Day after day, mile after mile, and weight after weight, Mike thought he was making strides toward greatness, when in fact, he was deepening bad mental habits of ego-oriented golf that would influence him in the future. Mike was trying to improve at golf for other people, not for himself. And when he returned to competition, he was playing to an audience that didn't really care.

Because Mike had spent so much time deepening the creases of bad mental habits, the process of reorienting his perspective to a mastery approach took time and patience, the way that replacing bad habits always does. Developing a mastery approach became a day-to-day process of monitoring those cues to which he reacted so powerfully. Mike had to now be careful how he reacted to compliments and recognition. It was difficult for him to not let himself feel good when he hit a good shot in front of people. After all, it was that very recognition that he had worked so hard to regain during the comeback, and it was, after all, a deeply ingrained habit.

In time he realized the importance of making golf a personal endeavor, and playing to achieve self-set goals and personal expectations. Mike began to understand that giving someone the power to elevate your confidence through their praise also gives them the power to sting you with their criticism. He also realized that the one person who really understood his game better than anyone was himself. Thus, *he* was the best judge of how good or bad a shot was. He was still polite when people complimented a good shot, but by and large, he listened more to himself and his swing coach than to casual observers.

Mike also had to begin thinking about rankings, cuts, and competition differently. Playing golf with the mindset of beating another golfer meant that he would essentially be aiming at a moving target, because he had no way of predicting what a golfer was going to shoot on any given hole. By trying to play against other players, golfers actually build uncertainty right into their golf game. So Mike had to learn to play his own game again, which meant he had to develop a strategy ahead of time of how he would play each hole and each shot. This kept his mind focused on the course, not on the competition.

I helped Mike better understand how mastery-oriented golfers think about practice and how he could build mastery right into his practice sessions. We discussed how to compartmentalize (mentally separate the tournament from the golf course where the tournament is held). We discussed strategies to remain fully involved in each shot regardless of leaderboard, stature of the field, or consequences of the shot. I gave Mike interviews that I'd collected with mastery golfers so he could begin seeing the thinking patterns of Hogan, Nicklaus, and Woods for himself.

One of the things that Mike had to understand, and that all golfers have to understand, is that golf is a game of *irony*. To shoot low scores, you cannot remain squarely focused on shooting low scores. To beat other players, you cannot remain squarely focused on beating other players. To win tournaments, you cannot remain squarely focused on winning tournaments. And to gain the admiration and respect of other golfers, you cannot play golf for the reason of gaining respect and admiration of other golfers. Golf must be played the right way and for the right reasons. Awards, recognition, and prizes, if they are to be had, must follow as natural consequences of hitting great shots. The ability to hit great shots must come from passion for learning and playing the game.

Mike's story is still being written. He has begun to understand the ironies of golf and has begun to approach golf from a mastery perspective. He still finds his mind distracted sometimes with ego-oriented thoughts, but those thoughts do not cripple him as they once did. Mike is definitely having more fun at golf now than he was having before, and this fun translates across practice sessions, recreational rounds, and competitive rounds of golf. The first thing he does on arriving at the course for tournaments is to introduce himself to the golf course. Now he knows what Hogan, Nicklaus, and Woods always knew. That golf is a private matter between two players: a golfer and the course on which he's playing.

When you require the approval of others, you give them the key to your emotions—and you forfeit a fair amount of control over your confidence, too. Ego golfers view a bad round of golf as humiliating, debilitating, and embarrassing. As a result, they play with the ever-present sense that humiliation is just around the corner. That, friends, in a clinical setting might otherwise be described as neurosis; for our purposes, here it's called playing with fear.

For ego golfers, a golf round can be an emotional roller coaster—euphorically high at certain times, excruciatingly low at others—all depending on how they think they are being viewed and evaluated. (Note: That sense of evaluation isn't limited to outsiders, either. An ego golfer's self-evaluation can be just as destructive.) They move through the golf course trying to show off with good shots and trying to avoid hitting embarrassingly bad shots. Curiously, they have an equal tendency to play overly conservative at times, and wildly aggressive at others. Facing any kind of pressure, ego golfers inevitably must do a dance with the dreaded "c" word, choke. Whether they are trying to hold off opponents, protect leads, or play "just good enough" to maintain whatever slight advantage they have, choking is never far from their perspective. Again, you don't have to be trying to hold on to a one-shot lead at the U.S. Open to know this sensation. You can be one-up on your buddy on the seventeenth tee, or you can need bogey on 18 to break 90.

This difference between seeking approval and avoiding embarrassment can be well understood as the difference between "playing to impress" or "playing to avoid looking foolish." Spanish legend Seve Ballesteros once quipped that in the days when he was at the top of his game he would cry on the tenth tee because he had only nine chances left to make birdie. Now he cries because he has nine holes left to play, which leaves him nine more chances to make bogey. This certainly illustrates the difference between playing fearless, mastery golf or playing fear-filled, ego golf.

The confidence of ego golfers often fluctuates depending on the stakes attached to their golf, as well as on where they stand in relation to those stakes. Professional ego golfers can easily be influenced by the prestige of a field, the amount of prize money, their playing partners' scores, who they are playing with, or the attention and respect they expect to garnish depending on how well they play. For recreational golfers, if their boss is part of their foursome, rest assured that the confidence of the ego golfer rests securely in the boss's hands rather than in the golfer's skills, where it should be.

I once began a lecture to the Georgia PGA by asking the following question, which I believe is one of the most interesting in all of golf: *Why do competitive golfers typically play to the level of their "competition" rather than to the level of their "capability"?* As I hope you now better understand, different achievement orientations are often the reason why some golfers play to the level of their competition, either falling back to the level of those behind or responding to the challenge of those ahead. This is because they are not playing the golf course to the best of their ability and trying as hard as they can on every shot. They have not learned what Tiger meant when he said that "there are two opponents in the game: yourself and the golf course. If you can somehow combat those two, you'll do all right."

Instead, ego golfers in a tournament setting see other players as their primary opponents. For recreational golfers, they see the scorecard as their opponent or the esteem of their buddies or the admiration of those looking down from the clubhouse above the eighteenth green. Consequently, the well-traveled sports cliché that it is easier to chase than to lead is one that ego athletes understand all too well. Ego golfers have difficulty immersing themselves in the moment because their minds are preoccupied with the reaction to the shot rather than with the shot itself.

can i be both mastery and ego oriented?

It is important to note that these different orientations—mastery and ego—are not independent of each other. One can be motivated to win a major championship, enjoy recognition from valued colleagues, and *still* be mastery oriented. Differences in achievement orientations are always *differences of degree*. Everyone has it in them to be mastery or ego oriented at certain times. The key factor in achievement orientations that influence golf outcomes is how strongly golfers relate to each orientation, and in fact, every competitive person who works in a domain where excellence gets recognized is forced to deal with these issues. As a general rule, it is better in any achievement endeavor to be more mastery and less ego oriented because ego orientations often paralyze performers with the fear that their performance will not be good enough (i.e., *stage fright*).

Research in psychology has revealed that a mastery orientation fosters deeper processing of information, generates better concentration, leads to more enjoyment, and ultimately to higher levels of motivation and achievement. A mastery orientation frees golfers' minds from the worries that their performance won't be good enough, that they'll look foolish if they make mistakes, or that they will disappoint someone if they can't perform at the level expected from them. Questions like "How will I look if I miss this?" don't trigger apprehension or anxiety simply because they are not relevant to the goals of mastering their task and enjoying the process.

the pga tour's most important statistic

The most interesting golf statistic to the psychological observer is the "bounce back" statistic that the PGA Tour keeps. Bounce back measures the times a golfer follows a bogey or worse with a birdie on the following hole. In 2000, a year in which he won three majors, Tiger's bounce-back statistic was an amazing 36.8 percent. Better than one of every three times he made a bogey on a hole, he followed it up with a birdie on the next hole. In his nine seasons as a pro, Tiger has averaged better than 25 percent in the bounce-back category, finishing in the top twelve in the final statistics six times and winning the

cont. on next page

cont. from previous page

category outright twice. Greatness isn't about your makes, it's about your misses, and the number-one player in the world freely acknowledges as much, writing in *Golf Digest*,

I've hit a variety of snipes, quacks, and shrimps in my lifetime, and if I continue to play I'll hit plenty more. I realize that a poor shot is just a swing away. I also realize that, once I've hit a poor shot my only recourse is to hit a better shot on the next swing. In other words, I've learned to hit it and forget it. There's no sense dwelling on a mistake. You can't hit the shot again, so forget about it.

When adversity serves as a trigger for immediate recovery, that is psychological bounce back at its best.

Mastery oriented golfers do not typically see golf as a competition between themselves and other players. Rather, they focus on playing a golf course the way that the golf course needs to be played. This is a small but highly important psychological distinction. Trying to play against other golfers and trying to play a golf course is like playing entirely different sports. Each comes with its own psychological consequences. When asked if competing against Byron Nelson or Sam Snead made him a better golfer, Ben Hogan responded, "I never felt any competitive urge of one person against the other. We all played tournaments and tried to do the best we could every time we played."

It is for these reasons that I constantly remind the golfers with whom I work that they need to be mastery focused. I try to teach them:

1. You *are not* playing against a score.
2. You *are not* playing against a tournament.
3. You *are not* playing against other players.
4. You *are* playing a golf course, one shot at a time, the best way you know how.

Golfers with a mastery approach to the game try to play each hole as it needs to be played, to the best of their ability. They know that success on a previous hole does not mean much to the hole they are facing and that prior shots or future outcomes have little bearing on the task before them. They understand that great golf is the summation of individual shots and that every shot is a chance to get closer and closer to perfection. Because they view golf this way, they find it easy to immerse themselves in the process of playing golf, and they often concentrate to the point of ignoring everything around them. Golfers in a mastery mode are not competing against those first three things above.

It is the insistence on playing the golf course rather than other players that marks the difference between the top players like Tiger Woods and Vijay Singh and the rest of the field. They are driven by a motivation that goes beyond the leaderboard or the situation. Playing the golf course is the reason a great player turns five-shot leads into eight-shot leads. The truly dominant, truly fearless golfers play to the level of their capabilities, not the level of their competition. The effort and motivation remain constant regardless of where he stands in a tournament. Tiger once said, "I will try as hard as I possibly can. Just like I do every round. That's a given. My effort, that's a constant." Likewise, in the course of winning seventeen times in two years, Vijay strived to not let himself get caught up in the enormity of the achievement. He just went out and hit golf shots. The winning took care of itself. He said at the end of 2004, "Every tournament you start off even on Thursday, and whatever you've done a week before, you can throw that out the window. To me, every time I tee it up, it's a new event. You need 100 percent focus on that event."

That sort of dedication to competing against a golf course every single round prevents the great player, the fearless golfer, from the emotional and motivational differences most golfers feel between Thursday and Sunday. The top players' intensity, motivation, and commitment to each and every golf shot are the same on Thursday as they are on Sunday. They have to be. And a successful attitude at the start breeds success at the finish.

glimpses of mastery golf

Even top-notch golfers whose approach to the game is mastery oriented fall into the trap sometimes. Steve Flesch is a tour veteran and a mastery golfer whose key motivation for playing golf is simply "to challenge myself and see how good I can become." Indeed, few athletes anywhere are as competitive as Steve. However, for a round in 2000 he lost his mastery perspective and shifted from playing the course to playing an opponent. He went into the final round of the Disney Classic with the lead. In our interview, he recollected:

> I remember Disney two years ago. I was playing with a lead and paired with Tiger and Jeff Sluman in the final round and I was two shots ahead of Tiger. Of everyone to be paired with, right? I figured that if I could hold him off, he was the guy, that I would win the golf tournament. Even though I am the one with the lead, I am trying to hold him off. I was in control the whole day. I really wasn't nervous. I still felt like I was the guy they had to chase and I still stayed aggressive. I still didn't change the way I played. I played great. Unfortunately, Duffy Waldorf shot 62 that day to beat me by a shot. I shot 69. I did what I had to do but even though I stayed ahead of Tiger, I think I needed to keep playing the golf course to where I didn't just try and beat him. I do think I got to a point where I was trying to just make pars where I should have stayed just as aggressive. Played the course. Play the golf course and not another individual and I probably would have won because I had the game that day.

I use this passage to illustrate two things. First of all, how someone like Steve, who typically has a strong mastery orientation, can slip into thinking about results. Second, to illustrate a simple and rather obvious reason why playing an opponent often leads golfers to play to the level of their competition rather than to the level of their capability.

Now contrast this mindset with Steve's remarks about his first professional win at the 2003 HP Classic in New Orleans after which time he learned the importance of mastery golf. Three years later, Steve had learned a lot:

> The second place I had at Disney hurts a little bit because I played so well head-to-head against Tiger, I believe that was 2000 and Duffy Waldorf shot 62. I tell you, I said to myself, when I had the lead going into Saturday, If I can hold off Tiger for the weekend, man, I was going to win. I held off Tiger, but Duffy shot 62 and beat me. But, you know, today I just told myself from the get-go, hang in there. And today when I got off to that start—I think I was at 4-under or something, I didn't look at the board because I was like, You know what? Today, not that I'm infallible, not one of those *Caddyshack* things, but I was like, You know what? You're in a great frame of mind, let's just keep it going. Play the course. Don't think about the leader.

As noted above, I consider Jack Nicklaus to be the ultimate model of a mastery-oriented golfer. We've often heard Jack emphasize that he never played golf for records or money. "I never played for the money and I never thought about my place in relation to other golfers or their records," he's said. "When I turned professional there weren't those big purses anyhow. Back then you played because you loved to play and compete. That was the reward."

Nicklaus is in great company when it comes to his view of achievement, as most people who achieve excellence in their chosen endeavors relay very similar sentiments. For instance, at the age of sixteen, astronaut Neil Armstrong built a small wind tunnel in the basement of his home where he would constantly perform experiments on the model planes he made. After being the first person to walk on the moon, he refused countless interviews and media opportunities. Instead, he followed his passion for aeronautics to a small town in Ohio, where he took a job teaching engineering. He was a task-oriented man who pursued aeronautics because he loved it, not because he loved the recognition it brought him. Similar patterns are seen in the lives of extraordinary people like physicist Albert Einstein, artist Pablo Picasso, psychoanalyst Sigmund Freud, football player Joe Montana, tennis player Steffi Graf, and golfers like Ben Hogan, Tom Watson, and Tiger Woods. For people who achieve excellence, it seems that perks and recognition are nice, but they are incidental to the love and passion of the challenge itself. In concrete terms relevant to today's world, mastery-oriented golfers *tolerate* the media (and may even enjoy the insights of particular journalists), but they do not thrive on the attention and glory that comes with fame.

Nicklaus once quipped that "Golf is my love and golf is my

life." His vision of golf was clear from an early age. Nicklaus's teacher, Jack Grout, said, "For a very long period I don't think the young Nicklaus ever really thought about anything other than golf, even the opposite sex! And the better he became at golf, the more he thought about it, and the harder he was inspired to work at it." In *Two Great Champions*, Red Reeder illustrates Nicklaus's mastery approach to the game of golf while at the same time revealing Jack's indifference to others' opinions. He wrote:

> Jack learned that the real opponents in golf are not the other players but the golf course and oneself. The player must know the course. He cannot lose his concentration. Jack would get so set on remembering the course and thinking about his next shot that he would stare straight ahead with a stern expression. As a result, the crowds were not too friendly to Jack. He didn't get very many cheers or much applause. In their articles some golf writers made fun of him for never smiling and for wearing old rumpled clothes. Some of the fans even booed him on the course when he beat one of their favorites (like Arnold Palmer). Usually though, Jack was thinking so hard about his golf game he didn't pay attention to the crowds.

Jack Nicklaus, the model of mastery golf, wrote:

> Through that [learning how to read a golf course] came an ever sharpening awareness that one's true opponent in every golf contest is never another player, or even the entire field, but always the course itself. The only

thing a player can control is his own game, so concern about what other competitors may or may not be doing is both a useless distraction, and a waste of energy.

In October 2002, *Orlando Sentinel* journalist Steve Elling began contacting those golfers who were able to beat Tiger in head-to-head competition (it was a short list). He called and asked me what psychologically allowed a golfer like Ed Fiori to withstand the pressure that Tiger puts on golfers. I suggested that because Fiori wasn't playing Tiger, he probably didn't feel the pressure, so he had nothing to withstand except the challenging course in front of him. In recalling the experience, Fiori said,

I never watched Tiger hit a golf shot. I never saw a drive or an iron shot. I always looked at somebody in the crowd. I couldn't get caught up in Tiger, because I didn't want to see how hard he was swinging or hitting it because it's a different game, his and mine. You know, it would be intimidating to watch him and play with him. I played with him, but I didn't watch him. Maybe that's the secret.

Though Fiori's answer was short, it does provide a clue about what it takes to be a first-rate competitive golfer. His observation about playing with Tiger but not watching him is insightful. In fact, I think that focusing one's concentration on challenging the golf course while blocking out the play of other golfers is one of the keys to not only beating Tiger, but to consistently winning on the PGA Tour, the mini Tour, or in a local match with friends.

The difficulty lies in the fact that golfers too often look at a tournament like a horse race, when in fact they should look at it like a dart game. The media, fans, and friends can look at it like a horse race, like they do when they see Phil vs. Tiger or Ernie vs. Tiger or Vijay vs. Tiger. But in fact, the golfer has to think of an event, any event, as himself vs. a golf course. On that note, it is worth recalling that the word "compete" is rooted in the Latin competere, which means "to strive together" or "to seek together."

Evidence that golfers play their best golf with a mastery orientation exists both anecdotally and scientifically. You'll see examples throughout this book of how successful mastery golfers responded to pressure situations. What comes through in these stories is that playing the golf course, and shutting one's mind to things other than that golf course, is a key component of playing one's best. The psychological reasons that this is so effective, and probably why Ed Fiori was able to "beat" the budding superstar Tiger Woods head-to-head, are many. The obvious answer is that, when playing the course, one is playing against a constant, not against a variable. The difference between playing golf against a course, and playing golf against another player (and his fluctuating score), playing golf against the scoreboard or against the scorecard is akin to a marksman shooting at a still target or a moving target. Keying your approach based on others means that as the well-being of other players changes, even shot by shot, you are forced into being *reactive*, which leads to indecision, hesitation, and self-doubt. Same with basing your approach on whether you bogeyed or birdied the preceding hole. When this is your approach, your confidence rises and falls and you are subject to either dwelling on the past or worrying about future developments instead of immersing yourself in present realities.

words of a champion: chad campbell

Chad Campbell won the 2003 Tour Championship with a course/tournament record 61 at Champions Golf Club, one of the toughest courses in golf. Through 16 holes he was 11 under par. Two birdies coming in would have given him a coveted 59. When asked by a reporter after the round at what hole did 59 start creeping into his mind? Chad responded like a mastery golfer solely focused on playing a golf course as well as he could, one shot at a time. He said after the third round:

> It sounds funny, but I never really knew exactly how many under I was. I knew obviously I was playing good, but it doesn't really matter how many under you are. I kept trying to hit good golf shots and trying to keep making birdies.

cont. on next page

cont. from previous page

Finishing off the victory, Campbell had to turn aside the emotions of a player trying for his first win and he had to accomplish such a feat while facing the most accomplished field in golf. Wilt under the pressure? Hardly.

I knew if I played a good round I would be in there in the end. I just tried to stay focused and play one shot at a time, not really let myself think about it. It's hard to do, especially knowing that you have a little bit of a cushion on that back nine. And I just tried my best not to think about it. I think I did well staying in the present.

Furthermore, because confidence is a direct function of control, and we can't control what other people do, attention to other golfers undermines our confidence (especially when that other golfer is Tiger, who never plays the field; always the golf course). Finally, attention to what someone else is doing takes away from the most fundamental component of golf: hitting the ball at a specific target. If I am paying even a little attention to another golfer, or anything other than the target, then I am not paying full attention to the shot at hand. In golf today where courses get tougher and tougher and greens get faster and faster, even slight lapses in concentration can add up to big numbers on your scorecard.

recap

Mastery Orientation

1. Awards and accolades are secondary to learning, improvement, passion, and fun.
2. *Kaizen*—the goal of continual improvement regardless of performance.
3. Standards for excellence are *self-imposed* and *self-judged*.
4. Motivation to improve is an internal drive, not external rewards.
5. Obstacles are viewed as challenges to overcome (not threats to avoid).
6. Focus is on playing the course itself, not things superficially related to golf.
7. Competition is an opportunity to test and to perfect one's skills. The fun of championship caliber golf is to collectively challenge a golf course (not necessarily to win money or beat other golfers).
8. Poor shots lead to curiosity and greater motivation for improvement.

Ego Orientation

1. Rewards for playing are attention, awards, and recognition from others.

cont. on next page

cont. from previous page

2. Judge achievements relative to others' achievements, records, and expectations.
3. Primary passion is making money, outdoing peers, proving worth to others.
4. Obstacles are viewed as threats to be avoided (not challenges to be overcome).
5. Scoring well is more rewarding than playing well.
6. Scoring well is more rewarding when it is done in front of a crowd.
7. Competition is seen as a stage to prove oneself to others or to gain prestige. As such, other golfers are viewed as adversaries, and the greater satisfaction comes from beating other players, not necessarily from self-improvement.
8. Poor shots lead to anger and frustration (not curiosity and motivation).

I spend a great deal of time at golf tournaments, and I have noticed an interesting difference between mastery- and ego-oriented golfers. It is something you can look for the next time you attend a tournament and check to see if I am right. When they show up to a tournament, the first thing that mastery-oriented golfers do is study the course. They study the grass, the wind, the greens, and other course conditions. On the drive to the tournament, mastery-oriented golfers are eager to get to the golf course and they know that the competition later that day will be between them: the golfer and the course.

Conversely, when ego-oriented golfers show up at a tournament, their first stop is seldom to the course itself. Rather, they immediately begin to look for other golfers, the registration table, or friendly faces. They stop to talk casually to other golfers (usually *about* other golfers), to speak to media, to make an "appearance," and to let others know that they've arrived. On the drive to the course, their mind is occupied with whom they will run into, what the cut may be that day, and the prestige of the field. Ego-oriented golfers are usually not thinking about the course itself (while that is all mastery-oriented golfers can think about).

Ego-oriented golfers focus on these things in large part because they view tournaments as competition among golfers. Consequently, they seem to get preoccupied in the lives, stories, rumors, reputations, and records of other golfers. For mastery-oriented golfers, freedom from such distractions allows them to swing fearlessly. The mental baggage that comes with ego orientation sometimes makes those golfers tense, apprehensive, uncertain, anxious, and afraid of making mistakes.

EGO APPROACH ORIENTATION

Trying to hit good shots to . . .

1. Improve one's image in the eyes of others.
2. Secure bragging rights.
3. Beat other golfers.
4. Appear competent.

Ego Avoid Orientation

Trying to avoid mistakes to . . .

1. Avoid appearing incompetent.
2. Not worsen one's stature.
3. Merely protect a lead (when leading), not fall further behind (when trailing).
4. Not lose, not miss shots, not get beat.

the shift from mastery to ego

A pattern that I commonly see is a sort of psychological "shift" in golfers who begin playing golf for love of the game (a mastery orientation), but who subsequently switch to playing for extrinsic factors like bolstering their self-esteem, proving their capabilities to others, or making money (ego orientations). It often happens to junior golfers, especially those from "golf families," who begin getting recognition and respect from friends, family members, or members at the club because of their golfing ability. It also happens to college golfers who get to wear the prestigious badge of "campus athlete," and who then begin to stake their self-worth on that title.

Regardless of *when* it comes, the reason *why* golfers often shift from mastery to ego modes is because, in the world of golf, success often carries countless benefits. The world of golf is structured to draw attention to extrinsic factors, as money, rankings, and placements often determine exemptions, spots on teams, and sponsorships. As golfers begin to receive attention, awards, and accolades for their performances, they often begin to see golf as the vehicle for these rewards and accolades, and before long, praise and recognition become the primary motive for their play. And that is never good, because the mind then has to process competing thoughts.

As I have stressed, these differing orientations—mastery or ego—are a matter of *degree*. People are always mastery or ego oriented in degrees, and everyone is a little of both. What really matters as regards golf performance is the order in which these orientations fall, and the distance between them.

There is a cycle of cause and effect in golf in which negative reactions to shots result in lack of focus that leads to more bad shots. Achievement orientations are part of that cycle, and in fact, often kick a mental cycle off. The time to pay attention to achievement orientations is *after* a poor performance, when golfers are coping with failure. Ego-oriented golfers tend to inflict a great deal of pain on themselves after playing poorly. They drive pain deep into their minds, and usually leave the golf course as quickly as possible because they are embarrassed. Consequently, they approach future challenges with fear or panic triggered by questions like, "What if I play badly again?" Golfers who approach competitive golf primarily with a mastery focus, and whose ego orientation is a distant second, may feel a little pressure that naturally comes with social settings, but still be able to attend to the skills on which they have been working. Mastery golfers deal with poor performances by looking to correct the skills and mechanics of the golf swing or thought processes, not the emotions that accompany social shortcomings. As a result, they usually leave the golf course and head for the practice tee to improve their mechanics and refine their skills. They approach future challenges, not with fear or panic, but instead with focus and concentration. Even slight differences in ego orientations are intensified under pressure, and often are at the root of whether someone feels confident and calm or edgy and nervous in competition.

CHAPTER 3

Self-Efficacy:
The Essence of Confidence

They are able who think they are able.

—Virgil

I'll never forget Brian Kaineg. It was the fall of 1998 and I was a doctoral student at Emory University. Brian and I were playing golf and, bolstered by a book I'd just read on golf and confidence, I said to him, "Brian, you need to play with more confidence. You know you can't play well if you aren't confident."

Frustrated after a long summer of poor play, Brian looked at me and with an exasperated expression on his face he asked, "How can I be confident when I don't know where the ball is going?!"

As I reflected on his frustrated question, I realized that I didn't have a good answer for him. I went back to the book only to discover that it had no answer either. Consequently, I devoted a considerable portion of my graduate study at Emory to working with some of the best psychologists in the country and attempting to explore the minds of golfers in an effort to answer that question. I believe I have a better answer to Brian's question now than I did then, and I will spend this chapter providing what I hope you will find to be relevant and practical ideas about that elusive feeling commonly known as *confidence*.

The word "confidence" has been so often used in the world of athletics that it has almost become a cliché. Everyone realizes its importance. Golfers need it. They lose it. They find it again, and lose it again, and then just when they are ready to give up looking for it, they find it again (or more often, it finds them). They don't know why. They don't know where. They don't know how.

Some talk about the idea of being "in the zone," an almost undefinable state of grace that great champions seem to find when it matters most. In 2004, *Golf Digest* even tried to investigate the subject in a wonderful cover story by award-winning writer Jaime Diaz. Though the article detailed the advancements made through technique, approach, and technology, it concludes, "Though there's a good chance the zone will become more accessible, none of these advances guarantees it won't remain rare and elusive. It's a possibility even the most aggressive seekers placidly accept. Something elemental tells us that the mystery of golf was never meant to be solved."

Of course, I'm a big believer that mental success is not a

mystery. But that doesn't mean it's easy to achieve. It is the old chicken and egg dilemma: Confidence produces good shots. Good shots produce confidence. But which comes first? Playing well requires confidence. Confidence depends on playing well. Most golfers I meet have given up trying to understand the whys and hows of confidence and have instead regressed to just hoping it's there when they need it most. Yeah, confidence is a chicken and an egg: as fickle as a chicken and as fragile as an egg.

davis love iii: confidence confidential

For a successful golfer, confidence isn't just a word, it's a state of being. It affects every circumstance, every situation, every interpretation, every sentence. Davis Love III knows how much of a difference it can make:

> On a scale of 1 to 100, I would say my confidence is around 90 because it is not perfect. I think I see a few players whose confidence is always better. Guys like Tiger and Mickelson always have a swagger. Sometimes I doubt myself a bit, and get down on myself, so my confidence isn't a hundred all the time. But I think it's close to it. When I am not confident I'll say something like, "I wonder if I can play well this week." When I am confident, I don't

cont. on next page

cont. from previous page

wonder that. When I am feeling more confident, I am more patient and I am more forgiving. A bad shot doesn't stress me out. You don't ever hit a shot and ask, "What happened there?" Instead you let it go and go on to the next shot. I am more into just playing the next shot rather than dwelling on the last shot when I am confident. I say, "The next one I'll chip in. The next one I'll hit close." And I am also, it's easier for me to get going into a round mentally when I am confident, when I am excited I can't wait for tomorrow morning. When I am striping it, sometimes the eagerness gets in the way, but I have an easier time.

Another thing about confidence is that we can see it in others as clearly as we can see it in ourselves. Think of the memories confidence has given golf fans:

1996 Masters: Greg Norman losing it.

1999 Players Championship, eighteenth green: Hal Sutton rediscovering it.

1951 U.S. Open at Merion: Hogan masking it.

1975 Masters: Nicklaus protecting it.

2000 U.S. Open at Pebble Beach: Tiger exuding it.

2004 PGA Championship, first playoff hole: Vijay Singh seizing it.

Moreover, it must be had in the proper quantity. Have too little, and your opponent looms larger than he really is; have too much, and you attempt risky shots that invariably cost strokes. Defeat is imminent in either case. Balance has to be found.

But note that the word "confidence" can be used in all sorts of ways. It can refer to other people (I can be confident that Zach Johnson will win the next British Open). It can refer to the actions of inanimate objects (most days I am fairly confident that my car will start). Even when we use it to refer to ourselves, it may be unrelated to what we can or cannot do (I can be confident that my boss likes me). The confidence we need to speak about, the quiet assuredness that mastery golfers display, actually requires a different term. It's what psychologists call *self-efficacy*.

what is self-efficacy?

In a landmark book entitled *How We Think*, philosopher, psychologist, and master educator John Dewey put forth the simple but important idea that individuals evaluate their own experiences and thinking by reflecting on the outcome of their actions. In simpler terms, human beings have a tendency to get into their own heads. We all possess the "self-beliefs" necessary to exercise a measure of control over our thoughts, feelings, and actions. Through the process of self-reflection, we make sense of our experiences, explore what we think and believe, evaluate our own conduct and that of others, and constantly alter our thinking and behavior in light of those reflections.

Key to the process of self-reflection are the beliefs we create and develop about our own capability, about what we can and cannot do. These are our *self-efficacy* beliefs, which psychologists formally define as *the beliefs that people hold about their capability to organize and execute the courses of action required to manage specific situations*. Put more simply, self-efficacy is belief in our ability to succeed. That's the very essence of confidence.

Self-efficacy powerfully influences accomplishment. I know I can back out of my driveway without crashing my car, so I generally am able to do so without incident. I do not know that I can drive a stock car around the banked oval at Daytona, so I do not try. Each belief impacts the ability to act. I believe golfers' levels of motivation, emotion, and action are based more on *what they believe* than on *what is objectively true*. You will see, and you will hear in their own words, how many golfers are convinced that the success they attained was due more to the beliefs they held about their capabilities than to the skills they possessed, for *their self-efficacy beliefs helped determine what they did with the knowledge and skills they possessed*.

This relationship between confidence and performance helps explain why the success that a golfer attains is sometimes highly inconsistent with his actual capabilities, and why two golfers may differ widely in their level of success even when they have similar skills. Recall my earlier observation that, at the very highest levels of athletic performance, athletes simply do not differ markedly in their skills. We all know about highly skilled and talented golfers who suffer frequent (and sometimes debilitating) bouts of self-doubt about capabilities they clearly possess. We have also met golfers who are quite confident about what they can accomplish despite possessing a relatively modest repertoire of skills.

tiger's real opponent

There have been many times when great players seem to be lapping the field on their way to victory. Jose Maria Olazabal once won the World Series of Golf by twelve shots. Johnny Miller won the Phoenix Open by fourteen shots in 1975. Jack Nicklaus twice has won major titles by seven or more shots, including a nine-stroke win in the 1965 Masters. And of course, Tiger Woods has done it several times in his career, most memorably at the 2000 U.S. Open at Pebble Beach, where he finished fifteen shots ahead of his nearest pursuer. In these instances, it should be clear that these players at some point weren't overly concerned with their opponents anymore. Truth is, they probably never were. They know worrying about your opponents is a distraction. Focusing on things outside of your control (the weather, a bad bounce, your scores on future holes, etc.) is not a recipe for success. Tiger seemed to

cont. on next page

cont. from previous page
know that the key is to control the things you can control.
His words from a recent interview are a perfect example of
the mentality of the mastery golfer.

> When you get the top players in the world playing,
> it doesn't always mean that we're all going to be
> down the stretch with a chance to win, going head-
> to-head. In theory, it should get your juices flowing
> a little bit more, but the more you think about it,
> I've just got to go out and play my own game. They
> are going to do the same thing; they're not really
> going to worry about who is playing. I am just play-
> ing my own game, whether I am out of it or not, the
> game doesn't change. I still go out there and hit
> my shots. I've got to shoot the best score I possi-
> bly can that day. Hopefully, it will be good enough
> to win. Whether I am in the lead, or chasing, or I'm
> completely out of it, I always want to go out there
> and shoot a good round.

Psychologists contend that self-efficacy beliefs provide the
foundation for human motivation, well-being, and personal
accomplishment. This is because unless people believe that
their actions can produce the outcomes they desire, they have
little incentive to act or to persevere in the face of difficulties.
Our self-efficacy beliefs are instrumental to the goals that we
pursue and to the control we exercise over our world, how-

ever large or modest that world may be. A great deal of research evidence now supports the contention that self-efficacy beliefs touch virtually every aspect of our lives. Whether we think productively or destructively, pessimistically or optimistically determines in large part how well we motivate ourselves and persevere in the face of adversities; how vulnerable we are to stress and depression, and even what sort of life choices we make. In short, self-efficacy beliefs help determine the outcomes one expects. *People with strong self-efficacy anticipate successful outcomes.* Golfers confident in their putting ability anticipate, even visualize, making successful putts. Those confident in their driving skills expect their drives to be straight and true off the tee. The opposite is true of those who lack self-efficacy. Golfers who doubt their putting ability regularly envision two- or three-putting difficult greens. Those who lack confidence in their driving skills envision uncontrollable hooks and slices even before their driver comes in contact with the ball. And, of course, it's amazing how often the expected results are achieved: a low round for the former, defeat and constant difficulties for the latter.

perseverance

It is one thing to set goals, but it is quite another to persevere against the setbacks that stand in the way of achiev-

cont. on next page

cont. from previous page

ing those goals. Individuals with high self-efficacy view obstacles as challenges to overcome rather than as barriers to avoid. For example, behind every great success story in the history of human achievement is a resilient sense of self-efficacy. The number of examples are inspiring.

- Thomas Edison's teachers said he was "too stupid to learn anything." He was fired from his first two jobs for being "nonproductive." As an inventor, Edison made 1,000 unsuccessful attempts at inventing the light bulb. When a reporter asked, "How did it feel to fail 1,000 times?" Edison cleverly replied, "I didn't fail 1,000 times. The light bulb was an invention with 1,000 steps."

- Henry Ford failed and went broke five times before he succeeded.

- As a young man, Abraham Lincoln went to war a captain and returned a private. Afterward, he was a failure as a businessman. As a lawyer in Springfield, he was too impractical and temperamental to be a success. He turned to politics and was defeated in his first try for the legislature, again defeated in his first attempt to be nominated for Congress, defeated in his application to be commissioner of the General Land Office, defeated in the senatorial election of 1854, defeated in his efforts for the vice presidency in 1856, and defeated in the senatorial election of

cont. on next page

cont. from previous page

1858. At about that time, he wrote in a letter to a friend, "I am now the most miserable man living. If what I feel were equally distributed to the whole human family, there would not be one cheerful face on the earth." Two years later he was elected president.

- Albert Einstein did not speak until he was four years old and did not read until he was seven. His parents thought he was "subnormal," and one of his teachers described him as "mentally slow, unsociable, and adrift forever in foolish dreams." He was expelled from school and was refused admittance to the Zurich Polytechnic School. He did eventually learn to speak and read. Even to do a little math.

- Van Gogh sold only one painting during his life. And this to the sister of one of his friends for $50.

- Baseball great Derek Jeter went 0 for 14 in his first 14 at bats as a pro. Hank Aaron went 0 for 5 in his first game with the Milwaukee Braves.

- Coaches Tom Landry, Chuck Noll, Bill Walsh, and Jimmy Johnson accounted for eleven of the nineteen Super Bowl victories from 1974 to 1993. They also share the distinction of having the worst records of first-season head coaches in NFL history. Their collective record as first-year coaches was 1 win and 45 losses.

cont. on next page

cont. from previous page

- An expert said of Vince Lombardi: "He possesses minimal football knowledge and lacks motivation." Lombardi would later write, "It's not whether you get knocked down; it's whether you get back up."

- Babe Ruth is famous for his past home run record, but for decades he also held the record for strikeouts. He hit 714 home runs and struck out 1,330 times in his career (about which he said, "Every strike brings me closer to the next home run"). College basketball coach John Wooden once explained that winners make the most errors.

- The great tennis champion Stan Smith was rejected as a ball boy for a Davis Cup tennis match because he was "too awkward and clumsy." He went on to win Wimbledon and the U.S. Open. And, incidentally, he led the U.S. team to eight Davis Cup victories.

- Johnny Unitas's first pass in the NFL was intercepted and returned for a touchdown. Joe Montana's first pass was also intercepted. And while we're on quarterbacks, during his first season Troy Aikman threw twice as many interceptions (18) as touchdowns (9), and he didn't win a single game.

- Michael Jordan and Bob Cousy were each cut from their high school basketball teams.

- Cyclist Lance Armstrong was cut from his high school

cont. on next page

cont. from previous page

football and swim teams. He turned to cycling and in his first race as a professional, he finished dead last. He endured the next five years of being despised by the European racing community, who would put tacks and glass in the road hoping he'd pop a tire. His first five attempts at the Tour de France resulted in dropping out because he couldn't finish the race. After surviving stage three cancer and trying to mount a comeback, he was turned down by every single sponsor he contacted (one sponsor remarked, "That guy will never race again"). In 2004, Lance Armstrong won his sixth Tour de France in a row!

As these examples suggest, healthy, hearty, and resilient beliefs in one's abilities serve as buffers between failure and eventual success. They foster the determination to keep working in the absence of immediate or sometimes even remote rewards.

Self-efficacy differs from what people refer to as "self-esteem." Particularly in today's world, self-esteem has come to represent the feeling that one has about one's self. When you hear on television that someone has "low self-esteem," you automatically get an image of someone who doesn't like himself very much, someone with a low sense of self-worth, someone who feels unvalued. Such a person clearly needs attention and affection, perhaps even a little sympathy.

Self-esteem is an emotional judgment that speaks to how people "feel" about themselves, perhaps even whether they like themselves or not. Self-efficacy is different in that it is a cognitive judgment of what a person believes he can or cannot accomplish, independent of how he feels about the task. I have met my share of golfers who, for varied reasons, have very low self-esteem (they don't feel very good about themselves). In some cases, these golfers have powerful personal problems and problematic backgrounds of all sorts. Interestingly, despite their low self-esteem, many of these golfers possess rather strong self-efficacy about their golf skills. That is to say, they believe they can play good golf even though they don't like themselves a good deal of the time. Similarly, I have also met a good number of golfers who have wonderful self-esteem and are relatively content with their personal lives despite the fact that they suffer debilitating crises of confidence on the golf course. The key to successfully helping these golfers improve their performance does not lie in helping them like themselves more, as many television and radio psychologists might recommend. Rather, helping golfers improve their performance means helping them develop confidence in their ability to manage themselves and their thoughts so that they can produce the type of golf required to be successful when it counts, the type of golf they clearly have the capability to produce.

david toms and confidence grade

The power of a strong sense of self-efficacy isn't a constant even for an accomplished tour pro. David Toms knows that there are times that his confidence isn't strong enough, but he also knows that maintaining a strong enough baseline prevents disappointment from turning into disaster. I spoke with him during one of those lulls, and his assessment of himself and those around him illustrated how the game in your head holds power over the game in your hands.

On a scale from zero to one hundred, my confidence is probably about an 80 right now. If I'd won already this year I'd give you a 90, but that self-doubt is there a little bit because I haven't quite gotten the job done when I've had the opportunity. The difference between 80 and 95 is that, when your confidence is that high, you believe that nothing can happen that will keep you from playing well. *And I mean nothing.* You can run out of gas on the way to the golf course, and it is as if that was part of the plan. Running out of gas doesn't phase you. Nothing does. When your confidence is that high, even if you hit a bad shot—which I'd be surprised if you did—but no question about it, you would bounce back quickly. You would think of

cont. on next page

cont. from previous page

those mistakes differently and tell yourself "Ah, you can expect a couple of those. I better try to make some birdies," rather than telling yourself, "Here we go again" or "How could you have made that mistake?" When you're confident, mistakes don't affect you really. They just don't linger. Confidence protects you from that, and from making things linger.

I played with a guy this week and he hit it out of bounds on number 7, and made double. He never recovered from it. He was in a bad mood for the whole round. Even after a birdie, he was still upset. He never recovered. When you're confident, you recover. Recovery is key out here because while you're dwelling on your screwup, another guy is thinking how he's gonna make birdie.

Going back to the chapter on mastery and ego, helping golfers is a function of first getting their minds focused on the task at hand (playing golf shots to specific targets, one at a time) rather than on acting in an effort to live up to or enhance a certain self-image. The next step is often teaching them skills and nurturing their confidence to overcome whatever obstacles stand in the way of mastering their task.

If athletes could think any way they wanted and still play their best game, winning would be determined by skill and effort alone. We all know this is not the case as more confident golfers routinely outperform those who are technically and mechanically better. For instance, no one really doubts that generally Ernie Els has a set of swing skills superior to Todd Hamilton's. But Todd Hamilton won the 2004 British Open playoff. There are plenty of reasons why Hamilton won, but the biggest and arguably the most undeniable might have been that he believed he could. Also, there are countless golfers across America with driving-range skills comparable to those of many Tour players but who are missing the key element required to execute those skills when it counts in competition. Indeed, once sound mechanics are in place, it is the mind that divides golfers into different groups.

words of a champion: jack nicklaus, 1986 masters

Jack Nicklaus knows a thing or two about the importance of self-efficacy. He may not specifically know it as such, but it's always been a part of his makeup. Look no further than the 1986 Masters. Nicklaus birdied six of the last nine holes, shot a final round 65, and won his eighteenth major by one stroke because he approached the back nine with a profound belief in his ability to win.

Winning on golf's biggest stage at forty-six was as much about confidence and self-efficacy as it was about talent.

cont. on next page

cont. from previous page

> In the final analysis, there is no question that a genuine belief in yourself is the top requirement for winning golf tournaments. There have been many players who have possessed all of the attributes necessary to win with the single exception of sufficient confidence in themselves. An inner certitude about one's abilities is a golfer's primary weapon, if only because it is the strongest defense against the enormous pressures the game imposes once a player is in a position to win. Golf's gentlemanly code requires that you hide self-assuredness very carefully. But hide it or not, you'll never go very far without it.
>
> (Nicklaus, *My Story*)

One of the most important ways the mind influences golfing performance is by creating and regulating the beliefs that guide human behavior. Of all the beliefs that golfers can develop, none is more important than their belief in their ability to hit the shots required to shoot the scores they want to shoot when it matters most. These beliefs are referred to as *golf self-efficacy beliefs*.

Now, of course, it is one thing to talk about Tour-level ability. But what of you and your game? Think about your handicap. What is required to play to your number? It's not any set of skills that you haven't already displayed. What gets you to your number is largely a function of how you mentally approach your round and how you mentally perform during your round. That is something you alone control. That is where the average player needs to understand and work on his golf self-efficacy beliefs.

handicap index and self-efficacy

Golfers on the PGA Tour routinely wonder about their potential. They think they know it, but they are not sure. That uncertainty gets in the way of their executing efficiently under pressure. But average golfers should not have this problem. While uncertainty about potential is a problem at the highest levels of the game, average golfers should know their potential right to the stroke every time they step to the first tee. How? It's called a handicap index, and if you don't have one, you're denying yourself a key component to realizing your potential.

Dean Knuth, the former director of handicapping for the U.S. Golf Association, is credited with developing the handicap index and the concept of slope. Together, the two ideas made the portability of handicaps possible. In short, what slope does is let you take your handicap index from your home course and use it at any course in the country. Let's say you develop your 7-handicap on a very difficult golf course, like the TPC at Sawgrass's Stadium

cont. on next page

cont. from previous page

Course, where water comes in play on nearly every hole. That 7-handicap is in actuality a 5.3 index. Well, if you go to a much easier course, your 5.3 index may translate to a 6-handicap. The point is, whether you play a tough course or an easy layout, you know once you step to the first tee what your potential is that day. For instance, you know a score of 78 is well within your range.

Does that mean you should make decisions based on that number floating in your head? No, certainly not. You make decisions on each shot based on one question alone: What is my target? But certainly knowing your particular potential on one day lets you develop a game plan for the day. Just like when Frank Gassaway was playing for money and would not get discouraged by how the first hole went, so too should the average golfer not be discouraged by a bogey or double bogey on a difficult hole. Your handicap reminds you of your potential, and gives you confidence in your ability to score.

Developing sound mechanical skills is essential to any sport, but the difference between golfers at the highest levels has little to do with mechanics and ball striking. By the time they get to the PGA Tour, all golfers have the skills required to hit superb golf shots. Far more critical is their ability to execute those skills when it counts, which is nearly impossible to do when battling self-doubt. What individuals do with the skills they possess is in very large part a matter of the confidence they have in their ability to execute those skills. Performance in the clutch (in fact, performance in general) always depends on the confidence one has in one's capability, which is to say, performance boils down to one's self-efficacy beliefs.

How big a role does self-efficacy play in success? Well, consider that many of the closest observers believe it was the central theme to the success of the best player in the history of the game. I once interviewed Gary Player, and he spoke specifically about Nicklaus's place as the best of all time. He attested that during Nicklaus's reign of dominance, it was not Jack's physical skills alone that allowed him to consistently win golf's major championships. According to Player,

> I saw many players hit the ball better than Jack. But none of them had his mind. Nobody, and I mean nobody had his confidence under pressure. The bigger the stakes, the more confident he became. That's what won him the Majors and all those tournaments. And, oh boy, you could just see it! He was as confident as a lion out there!

Given two competitors of equal ability and equal amounts of good fortune on a particular day, the one with the most assured sense of self-efficacy will outperform the less confident one every time. That's true on golf's grandest stage, but it is equally true for you in your regular foursome next Saturday. Those who succeed are able to think in ways that help them make the most out of the skills they possess. I often play with golfers who have the potential to shoot good scores but who undermine their own potential because they lack the confidence to execute. As famed writer Alexander Dumas wrote, *"A person who doubts himself is like a man who would enlist in the ranks of his enemies and bear arms against himself. He makes his failure certain by himself being the first person to be convinced of it."*

the source of self-efficacy

More than any other psychological process, self-efficacy is the buffer that shields golfers against fear. I know what you're thinking, though. "Yes, I realize that self-confidence is important. What I need to know is how to develop it . . . and hold on to it!" The critical question for all golfers deals with how to develop and nurture the self-efficacy required to play fearless golf. Well, let's see if I can move you from what psychologists call *declarative knowledge* (knowing that it is important to believe in your abilities) to *procedural knowledge* (knowing how to cultivate and nurture that self-belief and, more important, exercise it when you need to). Let's go there now.

A strong sense of efficacy enhances human accomplishment and well-being in countless ways. Confident individuals approach difficult tasks as challenges to be mastered rather than as threats to be avoided. They have greater interest and deep engrossment in activities, set themselves challenging goals and maintain strong commitment to them, and heighten and sustain their efforts in the face of failure. They more quickly recover their confidence after failures or setbacks, and they attribute such failure to insufficient effort or deficient knowledge and skills, skills and knowledge that they immediately acknowledge are acquirable. High self-efficacy helps create feelings of serenity in approaching difficult tasks and activities. Conversely, people who doubt their capabilities may believe that things are tougher than they really are, a belief that fosters stress, depression, and a narrow vision of how best to solve a problem. Not surprisingly, confidence in one's golfing capabilities is a critical component of the success they ultimately attain.

bryce molder and the power of expectation

"Domination" is an overused term, but it is appropriate in describing the college career of Bryce Molder. During Bryce's freshman year, his coach asked everyone on the team to write down some goals they wanted to achieve. Bryce wrote down that he wanted to be a four-time All-American. Of course, Bryce took flak from his teammates for having such lofty expectations because, until that time, only three players in NCAA history (Phil Mickelson, David Duval, and Gary Hallberg) had achieved such a feat.

cont. on next page

cont. from previous page

But Bryce was unwavering in his commitment. He knew what he wanted to achieve and he was confident in his abilities to get there, some way, somehow. Over the course of four years at Georgia Tech, Bryce not only realized the goal of being a four-time NCAA all-American, he also capped a stellar career by finishing his senior year with a 69.43 stroke average (the best in NCAA history). Along with that, he tied the NCAA record with his third-round score of 12-under-par 60 at the Golf World Invitational. He set a new school record and NCAA record with twenty rounds in the 60s, and for his career, Bryce finished with the best stroke average in NCAA history at 70.69, bettering Tiger Woods's mark of 71.10.

I asked Bryce to explain the mindset that allows a person to realize those feats:

Well, I literally expected to win every single time I teed it up. My confidence was so high at certain times that I would enter a tournament and my goal would be to win that tournament by ten shots. Really. That was my goal: not to compete, not to just win, but to win by ten shots. I would ask myself, "How many do I want to win by today?" not "Will I win?" but "By how many will I win?" And you know what, when I didn't win by ten, I often won by a couple because that's what I expected from myself.

Before I illustrate that, however, let me take a slight detour to clarify something essential. A strong sense of self-efficacy does not in and of itself ensure successful performance. One can be highly self-efficacious and still perform poorly. All the confidence in the world will not help us when required skills are lacking. An underprepared but highly self-efficacious golfer is a confident fool. As poet Shel Silverstein wrote, "If the track is tough and the hill is rough, thinking you can just ain't enough." Even "luck" can play havoc with our mind. Clearly, the beliefs that we hold about ourselves can never be expected to be ends in themselves. Belief and reality must always be in concert, and so the confidence we have in our abilities must always be a reasonable reflection of the abilities we actually possess, regarding the task at hand.

Psychologists believe that successful functioning is typically best served by reasonably accurate efficacy appraisals. In other words, I make a lot of two-foot putts because I attempt two-foot putts knowing I can make two-foot putts. They also believe that the most functional efficacy beliefs are those that slightly exceed what one can actually accomplish, for this overestimation serves to increase effort and persistence. In school, most students are overconfident about their academic capabilities. This means that we should expect that a reasonable amount of overconfidence about one's golf game is rather a healthy thing. After all, the more confidence you have that you can succeed, the harder you're likely to try when obstacles rear their ugly head.

survival stories from the pga tour

- As a junior, Scott McCarron was kicked off the UCLA golf team, lost his scholarship, and returned the following year as a walk-on putting left-handed as an attempt to cure the yips. After graduation, he joined a business venture with his father that failed and broke them both. After taking out an $8,000 loan, he failed to get through Qualifying School the next two years. In 1996, in debt and on the verge of bankruptcy, he won a tournament (and $270k) in New Orleans. Through 2004, he had earned over $7 million on the PGA Tour, had secured three victories, and contended in several of golf's majors.

- When Bob Jones first came out to watch Jack Nicklaus play the twelfth at Augusta, the notoriously cool, calm Jack was so nervous that he proceeded to shank his shot right over Bob Jones's head. Of course, Jack rebounded quickly and went on to win seventy tournaments including eighteen major championships, six of them Masters.

- After being struck by lightning as an amateur golfer in South Africa, Retief Goosen had to overcome an array of ongoing health hazards. If that weren't enough, he suffered a broken left arm in a skiing accident in Switzerland prior to the 1999 golf

cont. on next page

cont. from previous page

season. That year he went on to beat Sergio Garcia in the World Matchplay Championships, had eleven successive wins in the Dunhill Cup, and captured the Novotel Perrier Open. He also won the 2001 U.S. Open.

- At the Milwaukee Open, Tiger Woods's first tournament as a professional, he recalled being "so scared I couldn't breathe." He parred the subsequent hole, finished tied for fortieth, and went on to win two tournaments in the next two months and earn his tour card quicker than any first-year pro in history.

- After three lukewarm seasons on the PGA Tour, 1983–85, Tom Lehman spent the rest of the decade trying to grind out a living golfing in Asia, South Africa, and elsewhere. He finally won his first PGA victory in 1994 and has since been a regular contender on Tour who has won five championships including the 1996 British Open and Tour Championship.

- After a stellar 1994 season in which he won the Masters, Jose Maria Olazabal was forced to withdraw from the Ryder Cup due to severe foot pain, after which he was diagnosed with rheumatoid polyarthritis. He was unable to walk for eighteen months without excruciating pain and was forced to miss the entire 1996 golf season. He would not give

cont. on next page

cont. from previous page

up. He returned to golf after persevering through treatment and subsequently won the 1999 Masters and 2002 Buick Invitational.

- After emerging in the mid-1980s as one of golf's brightest stars, Hal Sutton went winless for eight years after 1986, with his low point coming in 1992, when his earnings fell to a mere $39,324. He did not give up. Despite dismal success for over a decade, his belief in his ability led him to work even harder. Finally in 1995 he broke through with a win at the B.C. Open and went on to win seven tournaments including a showdown with Tiger Woods in the 2000 Players Championship.

- At the 1990 U.S. Open, eighteen-year-old David Duval had shot three straight even-par rounds and then birdied the first three holes on Sunday to get onto the leaderboard. Upon seeing his name on the leaderboard he was so scared that he admittedly "went into shock." He proceeded to shoot 43 on the back nine and finish well out of the lead. Duval did not let the setback deter him. Instead, he used it as a springboard to winning thirteen PGA Tour events, including the 2001 British Open.

But how much confidence is too much confidence, when can overconfidence be characterized as excessive, and what are the likely effects of such inaccuracy? Psychological research suggests that the stronger the self-efficacy, the more likely are persons to select challenging tasks, persist at them, and perform them successfully. As a consequence, they do not believe that it is typically a good idea to tinker with overconfidence unless it is clear that such overconfidence is creating a situation where an athlete is so certain of success that he is minimizing practice and skill development.

dirty harry and productive thinking

Dirty Harry, the renegade cop played by Clint Eastwood that became one of American film's epic heroes, had famous catchphrases that punctuated each of his movies. One of the more infamous came in *Magnum Force*, where Harry repeatedly grittily grumbled, "A man's got to know his limitations." Well, I'm a big fan of Dirty Harry movies, but I believe this line to be sadly mistaken. At least it is for players trying and training and ingraining the habits of the fearless golfer. Instead, the fearless golfer strives to stretch his horizons—even when he is not rewarded. Focusing on your limitations most likely prevents you from maximizing your potential.

I remember playing with an average recreational golfer once who told me he never had gone for a par 5 in two. I was surprised. "I know I don't have that shot," he said.

cont. on next page

cont. from previous page

Now, on one hand, that's an admirable approach to the game because there are certainly too many average golfers who stand in the middle of the fairway 250 yards away from the hole and wait for the green to clear. But on the other hand, there's a little bit of fear there that needs to be overcome, too. In the end, I wanted to know how he knew he didn't have that shot. Of course, you don't know the possibilities until you try.

If you think you can drive 300 yards, what harm will it do to try and drive 300 yards as often as you can? Slowly but surely your own results will teach you how far you can drive at a particular time and with a particular club. You'll also be pleasantly surprised to discover that the harder you work at developing your driving skills, the further you will be able to drive. And, of course, it goes without saying that the more confident you are that you can drive 300 yards, the harder you'll work to accomplish that feat. Great coaches never tell athletes that they cannot achieve this or that. Rather, a great coach simply provides her athletes with instruction, effective practice, corrective feedback, and appropriate encouragement, and she helps them to maximize their potential, always raising the bar as high as is reasonable given the athlete's capability at the time, temperament, and level of commitment.

Rather than underestimating your potential, stretch its possibility. That doesn't mean overestimating your ability. But it does mean investigating that potential through prac-

cont. on next page

cont. from previous page
tice and preparation. Then, when you get to that moment of truth, instead of thinking of Dirty Harry's famous line about limitations, think instead of what it feels like to carry his famous .44-caliber Magnum, "the most powerful handgun in the world." That's the kind of fearlessness that can turn aside any obstacle.

When we tinker with confidence, we never really know what other self-belief or psychological process we are tinkering with. I suspect that confidence is the spouse of spirit. When both are high, the marriage is happy. Deflate one, and the other will surely follow. We should keep carefully in mind that the issue of balance between belief and reality cannot easily be divorced from issues of well-being, resilience, and optimal functioning. Lower confidence can result in decreased optimism, discouragement, and a negative outlook. Like the cute little bunny in the commercials, humans need to be energized in order to keep on keeping on.

Research findings support the notion that, as people evaluate their lives, they are more likely to regret the challenge not confronted, the contest not entered, the risk avoided, and the road not taken as a result of low self-esteem and self-doubt, rather than the action taken as a result of overconfidence and optimism. The challenge to golfers on this account is to make themselves more familiar with their own internal mental structures without lowering their confidence, optimism, and drive.

As Pierre Teilhard de Chardin once wrote, "It is our duty as human beings to proceed as though the limits of our capabilities do not exist." Robert Browning was similarly correct when he declared that "man's reach should exceed his grasp, or what's a heaven for?"

This is the basis of fearless golf. Through a fully established sense of self-efficacy, we can see that fearless golf is a faith in a vision. Here, everything that can be perceived is possible, anything is attainable. Playing fearlessly does not mean you feel like you can do anything, but it does mean that you feel like everything you do you can do. There is an important subtlety here: I do not jump off the roof of my house expecting to fly, but I do climb down the ladder without fear because I have learned the skill of climbing up and down the ladder. I do not all of a sudden doubt my ability to climb a ladder; rather my past experience and my attention to the task provide the confidence required for action.

Just as confidence without skills will always run a fool's errand, skills without confidence leads to an unwarranted self-doubt that will surely cripple our ability to maximize the skills we possess. Self-efficacy is the belief that quiets the mind, greases the turbine, and ensures that pressure allows a golfer to focus rather than fear.

These beliefs also serve as the lens through which we view the world and our place in it. For example, we all experience obstacles, but note how people can differently interpret those obstacles. Some see an obstacle as a massive wall that suddenly appears and cannot be penetrated or gone around;

others see that same obstacle as a challenge to be overcome, as mere speed bumps to be rolled over.

In golf, self-efficacy beliefs influence how golfers view and interpret the obstacles that invariably appear. Consequently, the beliefs we hold will influence how we will deal with those obstacles, that is, whether we will be paralyzed by them or persevere against the adversity that they represent. Because we cannot succeed all the time, self-efficacy beliefs also influence how quickly, and with what mindset, we bounce back from errors, missteps, disappointment, and the unavoidable bout with bad luck. And, of course, our confidence to achieve specific goals helps determine the very goals that we set for ourselves.

gary player and the 105 percent solution

Anyone lacking in motivation, short on dreams, and in dire need of a boost in their own sense of self-efficacy should spend a few minutes around Gary Player. Besides a career of great achievement in the game, Player stands resolute as an example of the power of positive thinking. Almost from the beginning and continuing through every step of his career, Player believed deeply in his own personal possibilities. He took complete ownership of his own potential. Player, at five foot seven, never would be mistaken for

cont. on next page

cont. from previous page

the most physically gifted golfer. Quite simply, he was too short to be great. He did not come from great golfing stock. His father worked in the mines of South Africa, and Player came to the game through the back door, not the front. And his swing was hardly textbook by today's or any other era's standards.

But Player was a relentless practicer, especially in the short game. He routinely would not leave the practice bunker until he had holed three shots. Also, decades before it became standard practice in the game, Player was a workout fanatic, driven to improve his chances of success by being stronger and fitter than any of his rivals. But standing supreme in his approach to the game was an indefatigably positive mental outlook. He simply would not let himself be denied, regardless of the obstacles he encountered. In fact, he asserts that he welcomed any hurdle. His words are inspiring.

> People who want to resist and avoid adversity are cheating themselves. It is how you handle adversity that defines you as a person, as a golfer, and as a champion. I see guys out here all the time who let the littlest things undo them, undo their confidence, undo their motivation. I say, "Get in there and play the game with some courage, man! It is part of the game to have bad times. It is built into it, I think, to weed the weak people out. Nobody

cont. on next page

cont. from previous page

has good times all the time, so get up and fight!
Show me some courage! Show me some patience.
Show me some determination, for goodness sake!"

Being from South Africa in the era of apartheid, Player
was often heckled by spectators who would charge at him
through the ropes and throw ice and even phonebooks during his backswing. But he would not be denied. He won
163 times in his playing career. He won nine major titles
and is one of only five golfers to win the Masters, the U.S.
Open, the British Open, and the PGA Championship at
least once. He was named to the World Golf Hall of Fame.
And all of those accomplishments started with a com-
manding sense of self-efficacy.

"On a scale of 1 to 100, I'd say my confidence was
usually a 105!" he said to me recently.

Ha! I think that has been my greatest asset. Like
when I won the British Open at Carnoustie in 1968.
I wasn't playing well until 10:30 the night before
the first round of the Championship. I was on the
practice tee at 10:30, and then I found something.
I found something! And I went out and won the
tournament. I found it at the last moment—at the
last moment—because I believed that despite my
troubles and woes, I would find it. I refused to lose
my self-confidence, and you have to continue to be-

cont. on next page

cont. from previous page

lieve, because if you don't have the confidence, no one is going to give it to you. They are going to try to take it away from you. So even when I am not hitting the ball well, I always tell myself, "It can change at any moment. Hang in there!"

In summarizing his findings on the relationship between self-efficacy and performance, noted educator and self-efficacy researcher Frank Pajares once explained that

> self-efficacy is as much about learning how to succeed as it is about learning how to persist and persevere when you do not succeed. Self-efficacy does not provide the skills required to succeed; it provides the effort, perseverance, and adaptive thought patterns required to obtain those skills. Thus we make a very great mistake when we endeavor to prevent people from failing. Failure, after all, is the price we pay for success. Our efforts are better aimed at helping individuals learn how to fail when failure is unavoidable.

Setbacks and disappointments are unavoidable, especially in golf, so the golfer who allows bad times to mire him in worry and frustration will ultimately limit his potential. Developing the beliefs necessary to patiently and optimistically deal with failure is a key ingredient to ultimate success.

The great misconception of many beginning golfers is that failing will somehow lessen or embarrass them (the mark of an ego golfer). For them, failure is something to be avoided at all costs. Yet, when I interviewed some of the top golfers on the PGA Tour, I discovered that they consistently not only welcomed failure but invariably pushed themselves sufficiently hard so they could discover their limits. These models of success viewed every challenge simply as an obstacle to overcome, as another mountain to climb, and they held on to the firm belief that failure signified that they were pushing themselves sufficiently hard. Consistent with Robert Kennedy's observation that "only those willing to fail greatly can achieve greatly," their mastery approach allowed them to view golf as a constant learning experience, and failure as an inevitable part of that learning and a crucial ingredient to the process of improvement. They would heartily agree with renowned author Samuel Beckett's observation, "Ever tried. Ever failed. No matter. Try again. Fail again. Fail better."

Rather than ignore obstacles or try to somehow remove them from the mind, self-efficacy gives golfers the means to effectively acknowledge and overcome the obstacles that accompany any round of golf. And as golfers know, obstacles come in all forms. Psychological obstacles are as real as mechanical or physical or financial ones. Self-efficacious golfers find the means to succeed when their putting stinks, when their short game goes south, or when, as happened to Greg Norman, miracle shots from other players make success nearly unattainable. In other words, golfers with a fully established sense of self do not see misfortune and bad breaks and tough times as evidence of circumstances overwhelming their chances at success. Rather, they stand self-assured in believing that they control the results with their reaction to circumstances.

Confidence Drill: Built-Up Obstacles

Philosopher and psychologist William James once offered up the idea that we all should "do something every day or two for no other reason than its difficulty." One hundred years of psychological research since confirms that the presence of challenges and overcoming those difficult obstacles builds confidence.

To build confidence, press yourself to try new things. That means dropping a few balls 250 yards from the green and seeing if you can reach it if you've never tried before. It means maybe playing a round with only a handful of clubs. You'll learn how to get the ball in the hole, without getting bogged down in the minutiae of calculating which iron is your 167-yard club.

If you don't play enough golf to where dropping balls or playing with half a set of clubs is practical, use the practice green as your obstacle course. Like the Tour players, try holing 100 five-foot putts in a row or holing out a half-dozen bunker shots before you leave the area. The point is you'll never need to make 100 five-footers in a row when you're really playing a round, but if you get in the habit of holing putts of this length, having one on the seventeenth hole in your next round won't be a new challenge for you. You'll have figured out how to get beyond that putt. You'll know you can do it, and knowing is the first step toward doing.

Self-efficacy most clearly demonstrates itself when golfers are at their lowest ebb. Self-efficacious golfers do not fear failure because they know that ultimate success is a function of how they deal with that failure. The term I heard over and over when I spoke with PGA pros was how they must "weather" adversity. Success is the result of learning how to cope with setbacks in ways that golfers emerge from adversity stronger rather than weaker. As a result, true competitors welcome adversity knowing that it will weather them in adaptive ways.

No human endeavor is better than golf at exposing a person's shortcomings. In that sense it is the most revealing of games. Regrettably, some golfers are doomed to repeat their mistakes over and over until they eventually lose their love of the game. Golfers who practice sloppily tend to play sloppily under pressure. Stubborn golfers who refuse to adapt find themselves surpassed by technical and technological innovations. Golfers who have bad tempers play badly on courses that require patience. Golfers who are too passive have difficulty tapping into what American psychologist William James called "the fighting instinct" required to conquer life's many battles. And finally, golfers who do not find effective ways to nurture their own self-confidence are doomed to be victimized by the type of paralyzing fear that leads to choking, and which ultimately ensures they lose their love for the game.

In fact, adversity is the very ingredient necessary to cultivate mental toughness. Just as strong currents yield more resilient fish, and resistance training leads to strong muscles,
adversity leads to mental toughness. On that note, the role of
adversity in golf is best summarized by Professor Pajares's observation that "when failure is normative, resilience becomes
second nature."

I urge the golfers I work with not to be afraid of golf's
challenges and inherent difficulties, but rather to acknowledge them and learn to deal with them effectively. In fact, to
welcome them. The golfer who cannot deal with slumps, mechanical and motivational setbacks, injuries, and life's day-to-
day challenges will never be a top-notch competitor. On the
PGA Tour as in life, growth occurs from rigorous challenge.
As Stanford professor Albert Bandura once observed, a robust sense of self-efficacy does not come from ignoring the
odds. Real self-efficacy requires knowing the odds and feeling
confident that you can beat them. We must welcome the tough
times and view them as a down payment for subsequent success.

nietzsche and chris dimarco

Usually, we come to know the benefit of adversity only in
retrospect. Maybe we should learn to take comfort in the

cont. on next page

cont. from previous page
knowledge that hard times make us better. We have to believe that.

Existentialist philosopher Friedrich Nietzsche isn't exactly remembered as a motivational speaker, but his understanding and assessment of the power of difficulty and struggle is more poignant and more succinct than anything you might read from Tony Robbins. Though his words have been abused over the years, when Nietzsche wrote "That which does not kill us makes us stronger," he was suggesting that the hard times fuel success.

Chris DiMarco may not be familiar with Nietzsche's writings, but he does know the power of perseverance.

"To be frank and honest," he said to me,

> in golf the biggest thing is you have to admit your faults. If you mask the real reasons you aren't winning and don't actually identify the real thing that hinders you, I don't think you are going to get better. You have to learn from your mistakes. I've just been able to learn from them. And let's face it, in 1995 I wasn't mature enough to be out here. I lost my card. My wife was pregnant with our first child and I couldn't even play golf, so I had to stay home, which in retrospect was a blessing because that's when I learned how to putt the way I do now and good things came of that.

It is not easy by any means to see discouragement as the doorway to hope. But try it. You have history on your side.

Self-efficacy beliefs act as buffers against self-doubt during the trying times that every golfer endures. During times when the game gets difficult, the thought of hitting a good shot may often seem as "remote as the possibility of me flapping my arms and flying across this room" as Ernie Els once said. At every turn, these golfers modeled Lance Armstrong in his bout with cancer, and "believed in the power of belief for its own shining sake." They drew on their beliefs in their abilities to overcome the odds and subsequently achieved notable degrees of success on the PGA Tour.

The vast majority of golfers will never compete for the green jacket or the claret jug. Nonetheless, all golfers are similar in fundamental ways: They are trying to become better at a game that they love; they battle mountains created by nerves and by the yips and bouts of bad play that they cannot immediately figure out; they lose their patience; they fight self-doubt and shaky hands. Whether your goal is simply to improve your game or to win a major, neither is an easy process. But rest assured that you are not alone in your struggle, and know that the way you handle yourself at the bottom of the mountain will determine how high you climb.

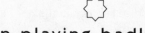

on playing badly well

When he published *The Modern Fundamentals of Golf*, Ben Hogan changed the way most people look at golf. By explain-

ing that the difference between good and great golfers is not
the quality of their good shots as much as it is the quality of
their poor shots, he allowed millions of golfers to become
more forgiving of their misses. In doing so, they also learned
to not dwell on their bad shots, but rather to learn how to get
beyond them.

It is this fundamental understanding that golf is a fickle
game, and that you have to play within yourself and your abilities that day, that mentally characterizes sound golfers. Great
golfers realize that they will not always have their best game,
and so they adapt accordingly. The better they get, the better
their misses, such that at the PGA Tour level, even their
missed shots are not all that bad. Great golfers or those hoping to maximize their potential have to master the art of what
Jack Nicklaus called "playing badly well."

This is where self-efficacy really shows up because one of
the most difficult things to learn in golf is to trust a golf swing
when you aren't hitting the ball particularly well. Indeed, the
natural reaction to bad shots is to change something in the
golf swing, or to become tentative and try to be careful with
the swing. An important jump forward on the road to greatness happens when golfers learn that caution can be imple-
mented into their strategy rather than into their golf swing.
You can pick more conservative targets, just don't make tentative swings. That's a delicate mental balance, of course, but
what it means in simplest terms is this: Hit the shots you know
you can hit.

Put yourself in this situation: You've popped up your

drive and are staring at a 220-yard shot to a green guarded by deep bunkers. The longest successful approach shot you've hit in the last two months has been 135 yards. What sense does it make to take out a 3-wood and try to loft it to the green? Not much. Yet many of us sit there and contemplate such a shot. If you decide to hit the 3-wood, do so with a firm resolve that it's a shot you can execute. But hitting a couple of short irons to the middle of the green and two-putting for a bogey is a good way to minimize the damage and possibly turn a 7 into a 5. Moreover, the stress of another bad number on the scorecard is reduced. That's the way to play badly well.

Like Ben Hogan, Tiger Woods recognizes the power of minimizing the severity of your misses. When I asked Tiger what was the most difficult part of the game for him, he replied,

> Well, I think it's interesting. If you're hitting the ball well, people think you're mentally tough because you're playing well. But I think where you see a person, what they have, what kind of mettle they have is when they are not hitting the ball well and whether or not they can still win a golf tournament and still put themselves in contention to win tournaments. I think that's where Gary [Player] and Jack were excellent. A lot of the great champions, that's what they were able to do. When you're not hitting well, those off-days, to still keep yourself in the tournament. Or even if you have a lead and you have an off-day, build the lead even though you're not playing well.

self-efficacy and recovery: bouncing back from mistakes

In natural sciences such as biology and ecology, the speed with which systems recover from damage is the defining characteristic of their health. For example, the health of ecosystems such as coral reefs, forests, and grasslands is measured by their ability to recover from environmental damage such as fire and pollution. Similarly, in the human body, healthy muscles are characterized by how quickly they recover from fatigue after workouts. Weak muscles often take weeks to recover whereas strong muscles begin the recovery process quickly.

The same principle applies to track athletes, swimmers, cyclists, distance runners, triathletes, and any competitor involved in cardiovascular training. For newcomers, a jog around the block can result not only in both sore muscles but also in cardiovascular fatigue. With consistent training, runners notice two things. First they find that they can run for longer and longer periods of time. Second, and more important to the elite athlete, they find that they recover more quickly from fatigue after they train. While initially it may take a full minute for their heart rate to get back to normal, with practice, the amount of time decreases so that mature athletes' heart rate begins to drop almost immediately upon completion of a run. They recover quickly.

A fit golfing mind displays similar restorative powers. Psychologically resilient golfers who are confident in themselves and in their abilities are able to quickly recover in all facets of the game. When they make mistakes, they are able to immediately forget about them and get fully involved in the next shot. In fact, the key to that recovery is their ability to immediately focus on the next shot. Again, remember the importance of the phrase "What's my target?" Rather than asking, "How could I have made such a stupid mistake?" they get busy finding the way to the hole. The psychologically immature golfer dwells on mistakes, beats himself up, and lets negativity, self-doubt, and anger infect his game. He dwells on mistakes and circumstances. He asks bad questions that keep his mind focused on those mistakes. He doesn't recover quickly. He even may not recover at all.

words of a champion: justin leonard, 1997 british open

Justin Leonard won the British Open in 1997 at Royal Troon with a 65 in the final round, rallying from five shots behind the leaders. Truthfully, though, he may not have won it with that score on Sunday, but with his intense, focused, and solitary preparation for the event. By coming to Scotland a week early and practicing at the course every

cont. on next page

cont. from previous page

day, he knew what to expect when the conditions got tough and the course got tougher. That resolve served him well after he fell off the lead with an over-par round on Saturday. He even spent extra time practicing after his round and was the last player to leave the putting green late that night. On Sunday, he had a little something extra that none of the others could find. It's a grit that his teacher Randy Smith knew well. Smith told *Sports Illustrated* after his pupil rallied that July day, "You put the big heat on Justin—the most people, the most pressure, the biggest scrutiny, the biggest chance for distraction—and he thrives on it. Put him in the middle of the ring, put him in the biggest circle, and he's gonna take out his bag of golf tricks and show you how he can use 'em. This kid ain't afraid of excelling."

From his words at his press conference that day, he was ready to persevere. He was aware of the moment, but he wasn't about to be overwhelmed by it.

You know, I told my folks last night that I'd come back from way back before.

I never thought there was too much golf course. The guys who were hitting it solid were going to do well, and the guys with the strongest mental outlook were the ones that were going to do well. You have to hit the shots. You have to stay patient, realize you're going to make some bogeys.

cont. on next page

cont. from previous page

I had a good warm-up session today, and it is so great to walk off the range feeling good, without really any swing thoughts. I was just going out trying to hit golf shots.

I think the difference has been my belief in myself, the confidence that I carry. If I'm playing well, it keeps building and there's more belief in myself and believing that I can come through in a really tough and clutch situation.

For the psychologically weak golfer, even slight mistakes often trigger a downward spiral. Focusing on a mistake leads to thinking about hitting a bad shot. A mind occupied with thinking about hitting a bad shot invariably leads the body to actually hit a bad shot. Bad shots often lead to anger and frustration, which lead to obsession with the bad shot, which prevents focus on the subsequent shot. The cycle is endless as one calamity simply leads to another. Like a nuclear reaction, the downward spiral feeds on itself. Prophecy fulfilled. And the instigator for all this mayhem can easily be one wrong reaction to a single poor shot. As Ernie Els admitted, *"When you're out there and on the verge, it doesn't take much to undo you if you're mentally weak. It really doesn't."*

Two things are evident in the way that PGA Tour golfers describe their self-efficacy. First, they indicate that strong confidence serves as a buffer against the pressure and fear that tend to overwhelm less confident golfers in the face of intimidating conditions. Second, champion golfers define self-efficacy by what it *is not* as much as by what it *is*. Confident golfers are able to see shots and hit shots automatically without thinking; those who lack confidence sense danger from the start, and even the most remote hazard can be enough to trigger apprehension and fear. A mastery approach to golf reduces the number of situations that golfers perceive as threatening and, therefore, as fearful.

Recreational golfers are not faced with the prospects of competing against world-class competitors in front of thousands of fans and a national television audience. Even so, they commit the critically unnecessary error of dwelling on their errors to a much greater degree than do professional golfers on the PGA Tour, who obviously have a whole lot more at stake. And, as we've discussed, the more focused you remain on the bad shot you've already hit ("How could I have made that mistake?"), the less focused you are on the upcoming shot you need to hit ("What's my target?").

Confidence Drill: Green Freedom

Anyone who has played basketball is familiar with the round-the-horn drill, where a player keeps shooting jump shots while working his way around the outside of the key with another player grabbing the rebounds and immediately feeding him a pass. What's impressive to me about this drill is how the player simply reacts to the target (the basket) and shoots, and how easy it is for him to find a rhythm and make shot after shot.

This same mentality can be brought to the practice putting green. I often have players I work with move around the green making putts from different locations at a rapid pace. What they need to be feeling is that same sensation basketball players learn of seeing the target and hitting the putt. By moving from putt to putt, a golfer learns to abandon all conscious thought, to simply rely on instinct and timing. The challenge is to build that sensation into your regular putting routine. It's what we see in the putting routine of a Davis Love III or an Aaron Baddeley. Each takes a final look at the target, then returns his eyes to the ball and without hesitating makes the stroke.

Automatic, thoughtless, efficient reaction to the target should be your goal. Practicing that feeling can help instill it in your mind for game conditions.

Self-efficacy beliefs not only provide the mental stability to remain focused but, more important, they ensure that the present is a "good" place not invaded by negative thoughts of self-doubt. Jack Nicklaus is an excellent model of high self-efficacy resulting in psychological resilience and quick recovery. Jack's mind was always forward-thinking. Whether looking for the next mountain to climb in the world of business or the next shot to hit at a tournament, he rarely dwelled on mistakes and momentary failures. His son Gary explained,

"Does my dad dwell on mistakes? He doesn't even remember them. Most of the time, when it comes to golf, he doesn't acknowledge them. In his mind, they didn't happen."

One of my fondest memories from the past several years illustrates Nicklaus's incredible mind, as well as the role of questions, self-efficacy, and recovery all rolled into one. I learned of this story while playing with him and his son Gary at Nicklaus's Muirfield Village Golf Club. It was a fun round of golf, full of chatter, conversation, needling, and laughter. As we were walking to the sixteenth hole, a long par 3 with out-of-bounds on the right, Gary suggested that I ask his dad about the 1984 Memorial Tournament when Jack hit one out-of-bounds while playing in the final round with the lead. "Well," Jack said, "I was leading the tournament on Sunday by one shot over Seve Ballesteros. The wind was coming from the right so I tried to play a high fade into the wind. I overcooked it a bit and hit it out-of-bounds."

I was shocked at hearing this because, growing up and hearing the tales of Jack Nicklaus in the clutch, it seemed that he never hit shots out-of-bounds, especially with a tournament on the line. Of course, my professional curiosity got the best of me. I asked, "How did you respond to that? What were you thinking after that shot?" What he said next illustrates why he is arguably the best competitive golfer in the history of the game. Without missing a beat he said, "I didn't have time to dwell. I was too busy thinking about my next shot. There were other guys out there trying to win the tournament too, so I wasn't busy asking about why the ball flew where it did. I was busy asking myself what I needed to do in order to win the golf tournament." For Jack, the amount of time between a bad shot and recovery was instantaneous. There was no dwelling. No asking "What if I blow the tournament?" He immediately got into the next shot by asking himself, "What do I need to do in order to win this golf tournament?"

Think about the questions you need to ask yourself when your sense of self-confidence is challenged by circumstances. For instance, after shooting 42 on the front nine, it is perfectly appropriate to ask yourself, "What do I need to do to still break 80?" The initial answer should be obvious: "Shoot 37 on the back nine." But don't stop there. Ask then, "What do I need to do to shoot 37?" Another obvious answer: "Do no less than make a lot of pars." Again, don't stop there. Ask, "What do I need to do to make a lot of pars?" Again, obviously, "Hit fairways and greens." And what's a good way to get started on that challenge? Simply put, what you must do is focus on the central question that guides every mastery golfer, "What's my target?"

self-efficacy: goals and expectations

One of the most fundamental contributions that psychologists have made to the understanding of human performance in recent decades is how people generally perform to the level of their (and sometimes others') expectations. Those who expect good things from themselves usually perform better than those who expect bad things. This is what psychologists refer to as the self-fulfilling prophecy.

Here is an interesting and telling study conducted in the 1970s. Schoolteachers were given the names of certain students from whom they were told they could expect tremendous intellectual gain in the coming months. They were also given the names of students who, for various reasons, were identified as having low intellectual abilities and hence were unlikely to achieve highly. The teachers did not know it, but the students' names had been randomly drawn. Nonetheless, at the end of the school year, the students whom the teachers were told had high ability actually improved not only in their grades, but also in their standardized test scores. Students whom the teachers were told had low ability failed to improve. This famous experiment has come to be called "Pygmalion in the Classroom," and its results the "Pygmalion effect" after George Bernard Shaw's wonderful story of Eliza Doolittle in his play *Pygmalion* (and subsequently the musical *My Fair Lady*.)

We all know that people tend to be successful in areas where they expect success and tend to fail in areas where they expect to fail. That mindset is effective in golf as well.

Of course, high expectations and goals are a direct function of strong self-efficacy in one's abilities. The lesson is that people in general, and golfers in particular, are usually capable of much, much more than they give themselves credit for. That is the prerequisite for taking your game to the next level (whether that level is breaking 90 or making more birdies). You first have to feel comfortable with the *idea* of being at the next level.

Research in psychology conclusively shows that performance is enhanced when a person sets goals that are high but achievable, specific rather than vague, and measurable rather than subjective. This is what Annika Sorenstam has learned from her great coach and teacher Pia Nilsson, who was her guide as she grew up on the Swedish national team. Nilsson instilled the idea of specific, powerful goals for each season, each tournament, and in particular, each round of golf. It was Nilsson's passion "to change the belief structure" so players could stretch their potential to new levels. The keystone of her coaching was an idea she called Vision 54, a belief in the possibility of making birdie on every hole. She once said, "Once one believes in the idea, as Annika does, then it is possible. It is a dream come true to be a coach of a player like her. Annika is always asking questions, and there is a lot of trust between us. When she shot 59, we knew it was one step closer to 54."

Such goals provide the motivation to practice, and they provide a standard against which to measure progress. They also keep the mind focused on the task at hand. Golfers with higher self-efficacy tend to set higher goals than do golfers with lower self-efficacy. Think about it: When golfers have equal ability, those with more confidence in that ability typically set higher goals and expect more from themselves. Such expectations will prompt them to work harder and remain more confident in pursuit of those goals. It is not at all uncommon for the interplay of high self-efficacy and challenging goals to trigger a positive self-fulfilling prophecy through which a golfer begins to realize his or her full potential.

One need look no further than Tiger Woods, who burst onto the scene in 1996 with the goal of winning every professional tournament he entered. Though many experts and media analysts called him arrogant and unrealistic, Tiger was unwavering in his commitment to that goal. He said,

> If I show up at a golf tournament, my number-one goal is just to win. To do whatever it takes to accomplish that, but to win. There's nothing wrong with having your goals very high and trying to get them. That's the fun part. You may come up short—I've come up short on a lot of my goals—but it's always fun to try and achieve them. It's just what I believe. It's the way I've always been.

His words uncannily mirror those of the man whose records Woods is chasing, Jack Nicklaus. Nicklaus did not rise to the summit of golf by accident or by divine powers. He was of course highly talented, but, by his own admission, not more so than other fine golfers of his day. What set Jack apart was not his skills, but his belief in what he could do with the skills that he had.

For me it comes down to having belief in myself. And I have always believed in what I can do. Even when I wasn't playing my best, then I had to root my confidence, not in my shots but in my ability to manage myself and my game. So if I am not out there playing my best golf, I know that. I know what my best golf is and what my best shots are, if I am not hitting the ball perfect I have to figure out how do I take 10 or 15 or 20 percent of my game away and play with the other 80 percent to maximize what I can do. People will say that is negative talk, but it isn't. It is actually more confidence because once I realized where my game was, I was able to manage it better and play the correct shots, knowing when to take risks and when to be patient.

One might well read this section and say, "Well, then that's it. I'll just set challenging goals for myself and that will be it." But that would be to miss the key point. Challenging goals and high expectations are critical to ultimate success in any endeavor, but rather than arbitrarily saying, "I am going to set high goals," they must always be rooted in the confidence that one can achieve them. And merely knowing that it is important to be confident is not enough to have a significant impact on either improvement or ultimate performance. The key factor in helping golfers improve their performance is to move from knowing that, to knowing *how* to develop confidence and remain confident in a game designed to challenge that confidence at every turn. So that becomes our central question: How can you remain decisive and full of self-confidence in a game designed to challenge that confidence at every turn?

The answer lies in understanding because contrary to how it may sometimes seem, self-efficacy does not blow in from the north and out toward the south. Once established, self-efficacy is a relatively stable state that can become a deeply rooted habit of mind. When it comes and goes, it does so for relatively clear and understandable reasons, and those reasons can be traced to four very obvious types of experiences. In order to understand these experiences, and thus understand your own sense of self-efficacy, first take a moment to write down something in which you are highly confident. Just as you did in the chapter on mastery and ego goals, take a moment to write down an activity in which you possess a great deal of confidence (it could be driving a car in traffic, being good at your job, giving a great speech, raising fine kids, or playing golf). Next, I'd like you to write down a few reasons explaining *why* you are confident in your ability to do this thing. That's right, take a moment and think about where your confidence is rooted. Certainly you are confident for specific reasons. What are those reasons?

Looking at your answers, my guess is that your confidence can probably be traced back to one of four key types of experiences. First, most people are confident because they have experienced former success in that endeavor. Second, it's possible that other people have often pointed out to you how good you are at these things. They may have praised you openly and frequently. Third, you've seen how others do certain things, and you know you do them as well or better than most of those you observe. Fourth, you are aware of how good you feel when you do these things. You may be emotionally charged or even psyched up during times when you do this activity. So your confidence is rooted partly in how good you feel when you do this thing.

Interestingly, the same reasons apply for activities for which we have little confidence (or for times when our confidence becomes shaky). We lack confidence when we have experienced a good deal of failure or a lack of success in a particular activity. Our confidence can also be shaken by hearing people tell us that we are not good at something. We can persevere for a while, but if enough voices point out our shortcomings we begin to doubt ourselves. When we observe others do easily that which we can do only with great effort or cannot do at all, it's understandable that we should feel tenuous about our future success in this or similar areas. Finally, if we find that we grow highly tense or overly anxious at the prospect of facing a particular task, we know that our body is telling us something that our mind may not yet understand. We can't necessarily explain why, but it doesn't feel good to do this activity.

Self-efficacy is always rooted in one or some combination of these types of experiences. Specifically and technically speaking, self-efficacy is rooted in one or more of the following four elements:

1. mastery experiences
2. vicarious learning
3. verbal persuasions
4. physiological states

Understanding these sources reveals why sometimes a pep talk bolsters our confidence while other times those words fall on deaf ears; why sometimes outperforming an opponent builds confidence while other times we can emerge from even winning feeling less confident; and why sometimes a rapidly beating heart means we are psyched up while other times it means we are psyched out.

Mastery Experience

It makes sense that the confidence we have in our ability to succeed at a particular activity is strongly influenced by how successfully we've accomplished that activity in the past. Successful golfers should certainly be confident golfers. Make no mistake about it: Winning is the most powerful confidence booster, and all the psychological card tricks in the world can't undo that simple fact. Winners know what it takes to win. Indeed, their sense of self-efficacy goes into hyperdrive the moment they come to be aware that they know what it takes to win.

Conversely, as we all know, there is no greater confidence buster than failure. But the sting of failure is especially devastating to those who have little confidence to begin with, for they are poorly immunized against the self-defeating feelings that typically accompany that failure. In competitive golf, the rookie golfer who is unsure of his competence is far more likely to encounter debilitating thoughts of self-doubt when he encounters a mild slump than is the veteran golfer who has successfully overcome such slumps in the past. To the habitual self-doubter, every missed cut, pushed putt, missed fairway, or duffed chip registers strongly in the mind.

Average golfers are particularly prone to this negative pattern, because obviously they do not have at their disposal the wealth of success that better players have experienced. To me, the challenge to the average golfer is to narrow the range of focus. They must learn to remember the good shots so that those are the ones that the mind flashes to in a crucial moment.

Those whose confidence is rooted in a great deal of prior success aren't battered by such pangs of fear in the clutch. Their success has strengthened their self-efficacy beliefs to the degree that those beliefs act as a buffer against self-doubt, fear, or panic.

Of course, those for whom success comes easily must also be on their guard. Failure is especially hard to digest when one is accustomed to quick results and easy success. A resilient confidence requires battle-tested experience in overcoming obstacles through hard work and sustained effort. Past difficulties, setbacks, and hard falls in pursuing the things we desire can be powerfully energizing, for they teach us the value (and cost) of the successes we finally attain. Such challenges simply provide us with the opportunity to learn how to turn failure into success by improving our skills and learning how to do better the next time around. Once we learn how to rebound from failures, subsequent failures get interpreted merely as springboards to future success. As the wise Confucius once observed, "Our greatest glory is not in never falling but in rising every time we fall."

When our memory is full of past failures, losses, and setbacks that did not lead to ultimate success, it is unlikely that we are going to have much confidence in our attempts to endure a current challenge in golf, be that challenge to hit a narrow fairway, or make an important putt. Conversely, when our memory is replete with successes and victories, difficult tasks do not fill us with apprehension or fear. Rather, the subconscious brain sends out a message saying something like, "You've succeeded at this before. You can do this. No need to worry, it's all under control. Just do what you did last time." Indeed, there is no better or stronger source of information about our capabilities than how we've performed in similar situations in the past, for our past performances provide a mental road map for us to follow.

A golfer facing an important 7-iron in a clutch situation feels confident and poised or nervous or edgy based on how he's performed in similar situations in the past. If in past and similar situations he has been able to successfully hit the shot, the brain sends out a "don't worry" message. This is usually accompanied by clarity of focus and a serenity of purpose, precisely the right ingredients required to replicate the previous shot.

Conversely, golfers whose prior experiences in such situations have resulted in disappointment usually feel the crippling anxiety that such pressure situations create. Though they may consciously tell themselves to stay confident or to stay in the present, their belief in their ability to hit the shot is blurred by images of previous mishit shots under similar circumstances. The mind sends out a "panic" message, and they are likely to begin to ask bad questions such as, "What if I blow it again?" Because they can only visualize previous disasters, the mind begins to race, and the body follows.

This is what golfers often call "getting in their own way." When they "think too much" or when their conscious thoughts interfere with their unconscious, automatic processes, it is almost always a function of low self-efficacy. Let me say conclusively that staying in the present does not by itself shield golfers from such experiences. After a series of setbacks and failures, the present can be full of panic and worry, so staying in the present is not, by itself, a solution. While staying in the present is a good objective for golfers, confidence is invariably rooted in prior experiences, so we need something to draw on.

Just as coming through in the clutch can enhance confidence, disappointing losses can cripple people's beliefs in their ability to execute skills they clearly possess. Unchecked, failure can flood the moment with dread. Too many setbacks and disappointments can result in real crippling self-doubt. Think back to football legend Vince Lombardi's observation that "winning is a habit. So, unfortunately, is losing."

Indeed, winning and losing can both become what William James called habits of mind, and they are each rooted in the self-beliefs we develop that guide us through tough spots and treacherous times.

Every golfer is going to have bad moments. The difference is some golfers will forget those times quickly while others will beat themselves up long after the moment is gone. Allowing bad experiences to fester is like playing a bad movie and watching yourself fail over and over again. Dwelling on failure often triggers a cycle of self-doubt and poor performance that in itself becomes self-sufficient. This reminds me of Hogan's observation that he had a tendency to remember the bad a shade more vividly than the good. This is a tendency that no doubt contributed to his increasingly poor putting ability later in his career. Low self-efficacy leads to bad questions, which lead to heightened fear, tension, and indecision, which lead to bad golf swings, which produce poor shots, which further undermine self-efficacy and fuel self-doubt. There are cycles of success and cycles of failure.

One need not have only supreme successes to develop a robust sense of efficacy. Because experience in any endeavor is a mixed bag of success and failure, individuals have the power to choose which memories they will attend to, the meaning they will give to those memories, and how strongly they will let those memories register in their minds. This is why how we *frame* our experiences is powerfully important to the self-beliefs that we develop.

Nicklaus once suggested that a golfer has to do everything

he can to protect his confidence, which is why, in his words, he has "made a lifelong habit of favoring the positive over the negative." Indeed, failure is so prominent in golf that Jack began to explain failure as "so-called failure" as a way to illustrate how golfers should think about mistakes as opportunities rather than setbacks.

In a book titled *Extraordinary Minds*, Harvard psychologist Howard Gardner introduced the idea of "framing" into psychological research. By framing, he meant the tendency for successful people to look at situations in a positive light and in a manner that gives them a competitive edge. By framing situations correctly, golfers are able to maintain their confidence in the face of any potential outcome.

david toms: underrated but undeterred

There's a difference between being great and playing great. As far as skills go, there will always be someone who does something better than you. For David Toms, his relative inability was never a deterrent. Instead, it gave him a game plan for optimizing his potential:

I think what allows me to be successful is that I know what my limitations are, and know the best way for me to play a golf course: where to take ad-

cont. on next page

cont. from previous page

vantage of certain parts of the course, where to totally shy away from. That is where I am good next to some other players who may not have quite "made it" I guess you can say. That's really the biggest thing is I no longer look for reasons why I shouldn't compete with the top five players in the world. I play with guys who hit it further, who hit it straighter, who hit it higher, who putt it better than me. But for me, it doesn't matter. None of it matters because I am able to take what I can do and put it together in a way that allows me to play my best. Some people don't get it, they can't do that because they lose their confidence. And that's the best thing I've taken from my experiences over the years.

Every day of our lives we each have the choice to frame situations in a manner that will either empower us and give us a competitive edge or disempower us and put us at a disadvantage. Our confidence depends in large part on our ability to extract the lesson from all experiences, good and bad. People have the ability every day to interpret the things that happen in their lives in a manner that leaves them either deflated or energized; doubtful or hopeful; stymied or empowered. Life always provides a curious mix of success and failure. The more we can frame our setbacks as learning experiences rather than indications that we lack ability, the more motivated and confident we are likely to be. Improvement at anything requires that we strive to do things we are not yet capable of doing, and so framing those experiences positively is critically important.

Framing is much like a system of belief. It reminds me of the sign I recently saw in front of a church: "Fear paralyzes. Faith mobilizes." We have no chance of acting positively if our decisions are cloaked in fear; believing in the possibility of a better way, trusting in the hope of expanding our potential makes success the natural result of a repeatable process rather than an accidental and unreliable occurrence.

nicklaus and framing

Few were better at self-motivation and framing in particular than Jack Nicklaus. One of the best examples of Nicklaus framing a crucial moment came at perhaps his greatest win ever, the historic 1986 Masters. In talking about the par-3 twelfth hole at Augusta, Jack recalled that

> The 12th hole at Augusta is one of the great par 3s in championship golf. The key is to aim at the center of the front bunker and choose a club that will get the ball just over that spot. I slightly favor the side where the hole is located. If the flagstick is

cont. on next page

cont. from previous page

right, I shoot at the right side of the bunker. If it's left, I shoot at the left side of the bunker. This hole perennially plays as one of the toughest on the course. When I was in the middle of my run on the second nine in 1986, I birdied nos. 9, 10 and 11 but I bogeyed here. That setback could have gotten me off my game, but I knew I was still in the hunt. I used the bogey to refocus myself down the stretch.

What a great example of framing! He interpreted a bogey as an incentive to refocus himself rather than as a negative event that could have undermined his confidence, his momentum, and ultimately, his great win that year.

In my interviews, a key distinction between golfers who were successful on the PGA Tour and those who were not was their tendency to frame situations in a manner that allowed them to be successful all the time, regardless of ball striking, mood, or how much they liked or disliked the golf course. Golfers who were unsuccessful tended to look for reasons not to play well, and they undermined their own sense of self-efficacy. They invoked every flaw, weakness, or shortcoming in their games as reasons they weren't ready to compete at the highest levels. Even before they showed up at a golf course, they would be talking about how they never play well on this or that course, how the course doesn't fit their game, or how some turn of events put them at a disadvantage. Conversely, successful tour players were able to look beyond personal shortcomings and flaws and instead rely on what they do well.

The lesson to be learned is that experiences alone do not breed confidence. Nor does success by itself result in a corresponding confidence. Rather, it is the "meaning" that we give to these experiences, and how we interpret success that ultimately determines how we face future challenges. Does a missed putt on the first hole mean you are putting poorly, or does it mean you are due to make one eventually? Do consecutive bad scores mean that you are getting worse as a golfer, or that you are improving because you are learning what not to do? Most golfers who get fixated on scores will tell you that bad scores are a sign they are getting worse. Great mastery golfers such as Bryce Molder will tell you something different. When going through a massive overhaul of his swing in 2003, Bryce chose to interpret bad rounds as a sign of improvement, not a cause for despair. "You have to learn your parameters with your new swing, so bad shots simply mean I am learning. Each bad shot I hit means I am learning something."

I frequently see scenarios where a golfer wins a tournament but loses confidence because of ineffective thinking. Imagine that? You win a tournament and lose your confidence? How can this happen? Through ineffective framing. I recall one year seeing a college golfer let a lead at the beginning of a day diminish so that he had to fight down the stretch to get the win. Afterward I spoke with him and he told me that he felt like a "choker and a loser." I could hardly believe my ears. He won the tournament! And though he won, he allowed his confidence to suffer a blow due to poor framing.

I also see golfers who frame situations such that their confidence is constantly being nourished. For example, in the 2002 PGA Championship Tiger Woods trailed Rich Beem by four strokes with four holes to play. Tiger birdied the last four holes in a row, a feat which he said, despite not winning, gave him a great deal of confidence. "To know you can do that when it counts is a great confidence builder." Even in defeat, Tiger found a way to let his confidence grow.

david toms and framing

You would think those who've been successful would get their highest motivation from repeated triumphs. Certainly, that is true to a great extent. But, as we've seen, no less a contributing factor to the development of a successful player has been adversity, even failure. David Toms shows how that vital sense of self-efficacy lets the ultimately confident golfer almost embrace the lessons disappointment provides:

I went through Tour school and breezed right through the first two stages. At the final stage, I was still doing well, and was in third place going into the last two rounds. Then I shot 78 and 80 to

cont. on next page

cont. from previous page

miss getting on tour by two shots. That was a huge setback, and the hangover lasted a long time. Then, the real rough times began. I went to Asia and played for a year, got back to the U.S. in '92 and then lost my card again in '94. I finally got my card again in '96 and moved up the ladder ever since. In retrospect, though, those years traveling in Asia, sleeping in crap hotels, being hardly able to pay my sponsors, those years were important for me. I needed them. They made me tough, made me hungry. They weathered me. And now I feel like, "Hey, I paid my dues. I paid the price. I deserve it. I deserve what I'm doing now. I earned it." I used to chase the golf ball around the world, driving from California to Massachusetts for a $10,000 first prize. Like I said, it weathered me. You can't buy those sorts of lessons.

Is it any surprise that when Toms won his first major at the 2001 PGA Championship he stared down the much more highly regarded Phil Mickelson? Is it any surprise that he won, even after being forced to lay up on the finishing par-4 final hole? Is it any surprise he rolled in a fifteen-foot putt to win on the last green? I don't know for sure, but I bet the answer might lie in some of those crap hotels in Asia.

Vicarious Learning

People do not rely solely on their past experiences as determinants of their sense of self-efficacy. After all, even in the face of continual improvement and numerous successes, people often lose their confidence. In part, this is because when competing people gauge their own performance in relation to the performance of others.

Recall the chapter on mastery and ego where we talked about the importance of framing golf as a game between a golfer and a golf course. Golfers who see their opponents as other golfers can raise their efficacy by beating those golfers, but their self-efficacy is also likely to take a hit when they get beat. Psychologically, there are two key problems with rooting your confidence in how you perform relative to other golfers. The first problem is that in competitive golf you lose much more often than you win. Every week on the PGA Tour there are 140 golfers in the field and only one winner. Even the best golfers in the world win less than 5 percent of the time. The numbers are the same for most contests across the world. When golf is viewed as a competition among players, confidence becomes reactive and unstable, but it remains stable and fixed when one plays the golf course.

The second problem with rooting your confidence in how you perform relative to other golfers lies in the fact that you have no control over how other golfers will play on a given day. Imagine shooting a 71 and losing your confidence because your playing partner on that given day shot the round of his life with a 68! When we root our control in the performances of other golfers, what we are in a sense doing is giving them control of our confidence. If our opponent hits a good shot, our confidence may suffer a blow. If he hits a bad shot, we may feel more confident because we are closer to beating him. But as time passes, a scale of our confidence begins to look like a NASDAQ stock ticker, very high at some times and low at others, all based on factors over which we have no control. All in all, there is no quicker way to undermine a sense of personal efficacy than to frame golf as a game between yourself and another player. Golf is a game that has to be thought of as a competition between a golfer and himself, and a golfer and the golf course on which he is playing. While it is often useful to use other golfers as referential comparisons to understand how easy or difficult a course is playing, or to gauge one's own progress, one should always guard against relying too heavily on other people's performances to inform their own sense of confidence. Rather, golf progress should always be measured against self-set goals and self-set expectations. At the end of the day a golfer's confidence should be rooted in his ability to pick targets and make fearless swings at those targets regardless of who he is playing with, and how well they may (or may not) be playing.

To understand the importance of rooting your confidence in your own play relative to the golf course rather than in relation to other golfers, recall the 1998 Masters in which David Duval shot a final round 67. After the round, all the media could focus on was how he came up a stroke short of the win. All the media could focus on was the loss. David Duval responded, "I just shot 67 on a very difficult golf course on Sunday at the Masters. It would have been great to win but I am not at all disappointed in myself. I played great today."

Hopefully you are able to see in this passage not only great framing but also the import of viewing golf as a game between a golfer and the golf course, and using self-referential standards as a measure of success. Had David viewed his performance as poor and had he interpreted the experience simply as a "loss," then his sense of efficacy may have suffered a blow. Instead he left confident in his ability to go low on Sunday at a major, a thought which bolstered his confidence and no doubt was instrumental in his 2001 victory at the British Open three years later.

Because golf is a social sport that is not played in isolation, it is often difficult to focus exclusively on oneself and the course. The best remedy for this remains a golfer's ability to get lost in playing a golf course. Toward that end Hogan used his practice sessions to "cultivate the habit of concentration." Consequently, his concentration on the course became so intense that he was often completely oblivious to many of the things around him. One time during the British Open he was asked whether a passing train bothered him as he stood over a putt. He replied, "What train?"

While the habit of concentrating on the course remains the best remedy for limiting the influence of vicarious factors, the best method of doing so is different for every golfer. Much of the success I've had helping golfers of all levels has boiled down to teaching them to teach themselves to ask the right questions as they play. Asking "What is the best strategy for this hole?" and "What is my target?" focuses golfers' attention on the course and on the shot which, in turn, means that they do not focus on other golfers and their performance.

One of the most fundamental and common mistakes that golfers make is to let the situation frame who their competition is. Situations vary constantly and golfers who let the situation frame their mindset find themselves often more involved in other players, their score, the gallery, playing partners, perceived impression they are making on someone, prestige, or what they don't want to do with the ball (rather than what they do want to do). They take their minds off of hitting shots at targets, and take their minds off playing the golf course and instead they think about other golfers and very often their confidence dissipates like steam. Thus I urge you yet again to be aware of the attention you pay to others, and to be aware of the influence that these vicarious factors can have on your own self-efficacy. Remember that, while it may boost your confidence to score better than others, it may also lower your confidence to score worse. Because we lose so much more than we win, viewing golf as a competition between golfers does not do much for one's confidence. Rather it is important that golfers always gauge their improvement and root their confidence *in their own progress* based on self-set performance goals relative to how they play the course.

VICARIOUS LEARNING AND MODELING. Let me now say a word about a positive aspect that comes with the human ability to learn vicariously. An offshoot of vicarious learning has to do with the role that "modeling" plays in the development of confidence. Modeling happens when we watch others perform tasks or engage in activities. Naturally, we tend to incorporate certain behaviors that models display into our own repertoire of behaviors. Modeling is so powerfully wired into human functioning that we often find ourselves copying behavior without even thinking about it. One need look no further than the tendency for teens to copy their favorite music stars like the Beatles in the sixties, Madonna in the eighties, and Eminem today. It is no surprise that legions of youngsters want to "be like Mike"! Parents are quite reasonably concerned that their children will emulate bad role models. Modeling can be a powerful vehicle for promoting behavioral and psychological change in all arenas, including golf.

Modeling in golf tends to take two forms: mechanical and psychological. In the mechanical sense, golfers often report that playing with certain individuals tends to influence the manner in which they play. For example, in his speech at the 2003 Memorial Tournament, Jack Nicklaus admitted that while he was still developing his game he would often try to imitate Sam Snead or Julius Boros. He observed that modeling their swings often smoothed out glitches in his own swing (or at least made it feel as though that were the case). Golfers on the PGA Tour often gaze at Ben Crenshaw, Fred Couples, and Brad Faxon, admitting that merely watching the smoothness of their swings or strokes somehow improves their own tempo and timing.

When asked the best way to improve putting, Ben Hogan suggested that one should "dine with good putters." In my mind, this is a particularly instructive remark that directly addresses the power of modeling. Of course, his point was that good putters talk about putting a certain way. They treat putting a certain way. They think about putting a certain way. They get excited when they talk about putting. They learn to love putting and, of course, their attitudes become contagious to those around them. This goes along with the dictum that "confidence is contagious." Insofar as possible, the competitive golfer should find individuals whom they think have great approaches to the game, and they should model them to the degree that the modeling improves their confidence. Since the tendency to model may well be wired into us genetically (monkey see, monkey do), I urge you to select a couple of golfers whom you admire and model the aspects you would like to possess. Keep in mind that, when looking around for models, it can be just as easy to emulate a poor one as it is to emulate a good one. Bad and difficult-to-shake habits can develop from ineffective modeling. If it is inevitable that we will pay attention to other golfers, and that this attention will influence our own confidence, then surrounding ourselves with successful models is a good way to maintain a high sense of self-efficacy.

Confidence Drill: The Power of Modeling

We've talked about how one of the ways confidence is established is through patterning our approach to the game after a successful model. Nicklaus modeled himself after Bobby Jones, Ben Hogan, and Sam Snead. Ernie Els modeled himself after Gary Player. Tiger Woods modeled himself after Jack Nicklaus. Adam Scott has modeled himself after Tiger and Greg Norman. Modeling does not merely mean copying another golfer's swing. Rather, it entails finding a golfer with a winning attitude and infusing your own mental arsenal with those winning ideals. When I've asked players to adopt the approach of one of their heroes to their next practice round, they often report back to me they are better able to cope with on-course adversity as their alter egos than as themselves. The plan obviously then is to start bringing their own approach in line with their hero's, so that the two become one and the same.

To get you started on that plan, study a player and learn the tendencies that make him successful and then adopt them as your own on-course persona. In fact, what may be even more helpful is to approach specific holes in the manner of a certain type of player. Maybe this tricky par 3 is played like a steady LPGA player like Meg Mallon, who plays conservatively to the green and then lets her putter do her scoring. Maybe this par 5 is played like John Daly, where a long iron approach shot is aimed at the pin and your sand wedge will save you if your aim isn't rewarded. In not too long you might find success and, more important, your expectations for success might be raised, too. Remember, modeling from others who have found success allows you to learn from their mistakes rather than having to make those mistakes yourself.

Verbal and Social Persuasions

As I've already observed, individuals' (including golfers') self-efficacy is most strongly influenced by how they frame the results of their experiences as well as how their performances stand up relative to the performance of others. The third way that self-efficacy develops is through the direct messages we receive from other people. Professor William Purkey once observed that "we tend to become what we think other people think we are." When we treat people in special and positive ways, we increase the likelihood that they will come to view themselves in positive and special ways. Similarly, when we disparage others, demean them, or belittle them, we rather powerfully ensure that they will view themselves as unworthy, useless, even unlovable. When recalling the development of his own confidence, Davis Love III relayed to me a story about his father that illustrates the impact of getting the right messages from others:

DAVIS LOVE III: I always felt that if I was working on the right things, or doing the right things, that I had the ability to win or to be a top player.

DR. VALIANTE: Where is that rooted?

DAVIS LOVE III: Lot of it came from my dad. He always told me at every level, "Do you realize how good you are? Do you realize how good you can be?" He was a good coach. Before Bob Rotella, he was a Harvey Penick disciple. I was always positive and I think a lot of that came from my parents saying, "You're a good person and if you work hard you're gonna get rewarded." I always had that confidence that I could do it or that it was just a matter of how I was gonna get there. Maybe that came from my dad's determination. Always telling me what I need to work on, but always in a positive way. What's in me, or what came from him is hard to say. I said in that little book we did that I hit it in the woods one time in college and Seve Ballesteros was winning Masters and British Opens, and I hit this big high cut 3-iron out of the woods about twenty feet from the hole, and Dad said, "You know that the two most exciting players in the world right now are you and Seve Ballesteros?" and I heard things like that all the time. Now was a lot of it BS? Was it a father's excitement? Maybe, but I was pretty good too. He didn't mind telling me that I was good. I think that it has always given me confidence in myself, and that I would either work hard enough or put enough time in or have enough ability that I could do it eventually.

Golfers must be aware of how verbal and social messages influence their confidence. Recall the chapter regarding mastery and ego goals. Recall how Mike thrived on the attention and praise he received from golf. Golfers like Mike who come to rely too much on the opinions and praise of others also put themselves at the mercy of others. If you allow others to raise your confidence with their praise you also allow them to sting you with their criticisms. Finding the right balance of whom to listen to, and when, is essential for social messages to increase confidence.

Surrounding yourself with people who are honest, but also positive, helps increase the odds of developing strong confidence in yourself and in your game.

Jonathan Byrd is one of the brightest stars on the PGA Tour. One of the reasons he is exciting to me is his confidence in his ability to be a top player. Where is that confidence rooted? Certainly it has to do with a combination of factors including mastery goals, prior success, and great framing. Another area in which his confidence is rooted is in the messages he receives from family and friends. At the 2003 Masters, I was standing next to Jonathan's wife, Amanda, as we watched him hit balls on the practice range. Recall that there were women protesters rallying against the club's all-male membership policy just outside the gates of Augusta that year. We were talking about the protesters when Amanda jokingly observed how inappropriate it would be for her to join the protests outside the gates of Augusta. When I asked her why it would be inappropriate, she said that "I don't think the Masters committee would appreciate the winner's wife engaged in a protest." She truly believed Jonathan was going to win the Masters that week, a message I'm sure she conveys to him all the time. She believes so strongly in Jonathan that it helps him to believe in himself.

Does it mean Jonathan Byrd will win the Masters? Hardly. But it does mean that it will be that much easier for Jonathan to believe in the possibility himself, no matter the circumstances. Recognize the power of those close to us to help us along. Faith naturally breeds more faith, so take advantage of others' confidence in you to restock your own confidence in yourself.

Lest the reader should feel that I am suggesting that the messages we give others should always be positive and flattering, let me take a moment here to speak about the cautions that psychologists offer about delivering "praise." First, it is important that positive feedback and encouragement should be delivered honestly and in its proper measure when the recipient is deserving of them. Providing positive feedback is valuable. We all want to feel positively about ourselves and about our capabilities. When it comes to golfers young and old, teachers and parents play a critical role in nurturing their positive self-beliefs. But heed carefully psychologist Erik Erikson's caution that

> children cannot be fooled by empty praise and condescending encouragement. Their identity gains real strength only from wholehearted and consistent recognition of "real" accomplishment. They may have to accept artificial bolstering of their self-esteem in lieu of something better, but what I call their accruing ego identity gains real

strength only from wholehearted and consistent recognition of real accomplishment, that is, achievement that has meaning in their culture . . . a strong ego does not need, and in fact is immune to any attempt at artificial inflation.

Praising a person for a job well done is an important way of showing love, support, and attention. Keep in mind, however, that praising with statements such as "You are terrific!" or "You're just so good at this" can often have the opposite effect you intend. Rather than praising for ability, we should make it a habit to praise the effort, persistence, and perseverance that it takes to succeed. Praising for ability tells a person that success is a matter of natural talent (which people tend to believe one either has or doesn't have). Praising for effort tells the person that the harder you work the more you accomplish, the more skillful you become, and the more you develop your talent. Nothing is emptier than empty praise.

Physiological and Emotional States

This chapter is about confidence, which, as you've read, is often understood as the antithesis of fear and doubt. While self-efficacy is about your belief in your ability to hit golf shots, it is also about your belief in your ability to manage yourself along the way to hitting those golf shots. Golfers confident in their ability to stay cool under pressure approach pressure situations with serenity, tranquility, and sharper focus.

The final source of self-efficacy has to do with the physiological and emotional states that are often interpreted as fear. When I say "fear" I am not only referring to that all-out, mind-bending fear. Note that fear exists along a continuum. Hence, I am also referring to the panic, stress, pressure, anxiety, and self-doubt that differently affect golfers as they navigate the day-to-day challenges of the game. At a certain point, everyone feels some of these nasty mental invaders and confidence-testers. It is how one copes with them that makes the difference. We have seen in Chapter 1 how fear physiologically impacts certain elements of the golf swing, how grip pressure gets too tight, and how the mind becomes less efficient at processing the complex series of stimuli that occur under pressure in a round of golf.

curtis strange: the power of history

Prior mastery experiences are the most consistent and immediate source of our confidence. Evidence for the transformational power of mastery experiences shone through my research. Twice U.S. Open champion and seventeen-time Tour winner Curtis Strange spoke insightfully to me about his career and how prior experiences made him confident.

> What I enjoy more than anything else is on the last hole, hitting that shot that I felt like nobody else

cont. on next page

cont. from previous page

could hit. And you know you're going to hit it. That is the fun of it, that before you hit it, you know you are going to pull it off. I remember where it all began: I hit a 1-iron on the last hole of the NCAA when I was a freshman at Wake Forest for us to win the tournament by a shot. I mean, I was so nervous I almost couldn't walk. But that didn't matter because even with nerves, I was able to hit the shot. And that shot started everything for me. Something like that is a big deal. It was the biggest thing in my life and I pulled it off. Wake had never won the NCAA with all those great teams they had, this was their chance. I hit it in there eight feet and made the putt. As it turned out, it did a tremendous amount for my confidence because it became the shot I always went back to when I was a pro. Because I was able to do that, I always felt that I was able to hit shots when I needed to.

Physiological changes by themselves are not the key factor in how a golfer performs. Recall that fear is inversely related to self-efficacy. The higher the self-efficacy, the less fearful a golfer will be. While the golfer with low self-efficacy has a tendency to interpret these changes as indications of fear, the highly self-efficacious golfer interprets them as signs of being excited and ready to go, often even as a sign of euphoria and mental sharpness.

There is a misconception that golfers like Tiger Woods and Jack Nicklaus have found ways to prevent these things from happening. Golfers often call on me to teach them how to prevent these reactions. After all, who wants to experience these nasty things? Regrettably, there is no avoiding fear. There is, however, the ability to cope with fear and minimize its destructive characteristics. While there are ways to quiet the mind and limit the degree of these reactions (for example, there is a difference between nervousness and panic and fear), it is better to learn how to play when these feelings rear their ugly heads. Every professional golfer, including Tiger and Jack, gets these feelings in competition. Recreational golfers know the feelings as well, especially if they are deeply committed to improving their game (as they certainly should be).

Tiger Woods acknowledges these feelings:

> Truth is we fail more than we succeed. You can't let those failures get to you, because they will erode your confidence and chip away at your psyche. The reason I've avoided those little devils is twofold. First, I refuse to give in to fear, real or imagined. I'm not talking about nervousness. I'm as nervous as the next guy every time I tee it up. Every competitor has a certain degree of anxiety. It goes with the territory. No, I'm referring to being afraid—either consciously or subconsciously—of anything or anyone. In order to be successful in any endeavor, you have to adopt a no-fear attitude.

The fearless attitude goes a long way in helping regulate how Tiger interprets those feelings, but notice that it does not eliminate the feelings. Perhaps the greatest thing I've been able to help golfers understand is that they should stop trying to find ways to not be nervous. Instead, they should find ways to hit great golf shots even when they are nervous. Such a fearless approach to fear proves calming. And as Curtis Strange mentioned earlier, every past moment of success positively influences the mind's interpretation of the next pressure-filled moment. Tiger provides insight as he remarks both on the power of mastery and the importance, not of sidestepping arousal, but of hitting shots with it:

> I like the feeling of trying my hardest under pressure. It's so intense sometimes, it's hard to breathe. It feels like a lion is tearing at my heart. But that gives you confidence down the stretch, when you are a little nervous, hands are sweating, eyeballs are bugging. You can summon enough strength to do it again because you've done it before.

Jack Nicklaus agreed:

> There is a difference between fear and nervousness. I have always gotten nervous at golf. I have played 90 percent of my rounds in major championships with a touch of tremor. There has always been some floppiness in my stomach. Moreover, I have always welcomed those feelings in that, so long as I am playing well enough to have

genuine confidence in my game, they will get me up, keep me alert, and prime me for maximum effort. Over the years, nervousness has done me more good than harm.

(Nicklaus, *My Story*)

Let me again emphasize that the key difference between golfers who are able to perform and golfers who are paralyzed by fear often has to do with how they *interpret* those bodily changes. Golfers who interpret these signals as a sign of fear or that they are about to choke will surely be emotionally overwhelmed and no doubt will choke. Conversely, golfers who welcome these feelings of heightened arousal and interpret them as a sign of enhanced perception and being psyched up are likely to improve their play. Only the beliefs in our head can help immunize us from potentially devastating emotions.

Great golfers are consistent in their view that golf presents a variety of challenges. They also believe that every challenge, even the "tightening" of the nervous system, must be seen as merely another mountain to climb. They do not try to pretend they are not nervous, nor do they seek psychologists who will help them not be nervous. That would be a foolish, and expensive, enterprise. No psychologist can prevent your nerves from doing what they do best, which is trying hard to get in the way of your peace and calm, especially at the most inconvenient times. Great golfers simply acknowledge their nerves and find effective ways to play well until they finally go away. Playing well is the best revenge against pesky nerves.

So we are led back to my old pal Brian Kaineg, wondering how he can be confident when he doesn't know where the ball is going. First of all, I'm not sure that confidence can be shored up and strengthened in the face of inconsistent and erratic play. But I am also definitely sure that you cannot possibly hope to play consistently if you believe you are going to play inconsistently and erratically.

words of a champion: phil mickelson

Phil Mickelson won his first professional major championship on his thirty-eighth try by making a birdie putt on the final hole of the 2004 Masters Tournament. He shot a tremendous 31 on the back nine to beat Ernie Els by a single stroke. That's remarkable enough stuff, but because of Mickelson's track record in major championships going into that final round, many doubted he would change the trend. In years previous, Mickelson had finished second three consecutive years at the Masters, he had lost on the final hole of both the PGA Championship and the U.S. Open when his playing partners had made long putts to win while he watched at the side of the green, and he had faltered in a slew of other majors when players like Tiger Woods had turned up the heat on the weekend. What changed in 2004? Certainly, he had a tremendous physical week at Augusta National that year, perhaps his best ball-striking

cont. on next page

cont. from previous page

and putting tournament of his life. But even more crucial in my mind was his mental approach in putting aside past failures to focus solely on the task of hitting the shots necessary to win the Masters. Even when he struggled on the front nine, catching a few bad breaks and even leaving a shot in the bunker on the fourth hole, he found a way to stay focused, stay positive, and play fearlessly on the back side. His smile never left his face; he was clearly embracing the moment and reveling in the challenge. What he said after the round was particularly revealing of the mindset of a fearless golfer. It's a mindset that has a foundation in solid preparation and a faith and a willingness to play without fear. These comments are a complete education into the possibilities and practicalities of playing fearless golf:

> Dealing with the losses time after time, it just gets frustrating. It can wear on you, except that you just can't let it.
>   I think the biggest thing for me was this offseason, spending the number of hours and days with [his instructors] Rick Smith and Dave Pelz to give me the direction. When I stood up on tee boxes, I just knew the ball was going to go in the middle of the fairway. Those hours of work and having that proper direction, I ultimately knew or did not ever lack belief that I would ultimately win.
>   I had a different feeling playing this week. I had a different feeling entering this tournament. I

cont. on next page

cont. from previous page

just had a real belief that I was going to come through this week. I didn't want to get too excited because I had had that belief a number of times before and it never happened. I felt very calm, though, and last night when Amy and I would talk, we were just very calm. We just felt like things were different. When I was out on the course, I didn't feel the anxiety of "Is it slipping away?" or "How is the tournament going?" or who is doing what. It was more like, "Hey, let's hit some shots."

I was very confident today that good things would happen.

creating self-efficacy

So Brian's frustrated question seems in retrospect more the problem itself than a step toward a solution. Simply by wondering why he lacks confidence, a golfer inhibits the development of that confidence he so desperately needs. Is there a solution around this psychological conundrum?

Of course. What we have to do as golfers committed to improvement is believe in the possibility of our potential. Instead of lamenting our lack of confidence, instead of believing the ball will go either left or right, instead of (in essence) accepting defeat, we must learn to challenge ourselves to be better. We must learn to narrow our focus to the specifics of the task at hand. We must learn to emphasize the results that foster this sense of confidence, the self-efficacy of a mastery golfer. Moreover, we must approach the playing of the game as a highly controlled enterprise. Instead of bombarding our minds with uncertain future results, we must learn to stay with the specific requirements of each shot, to see the shots exclusively and independent of all other circumstances. The tighter the focus, the greater the likelihood that we have set in place the foundation for successful shot-making. If we learn to emphasize the things that build this sense of self-efficacy and eliminate those things that detract from it, we begin to move forward.

Instead of wondering where this ephemeral sense of confidence might be, we do all the things we possibly can to create it ourselves. We control it instead of having it dictated to us by circumstances. The opportunity then to be a fearless golfer isn't dependent on anything other than our will to do everything possible to execute golf swings at precise targets. Certainly, a healthy respect for honing the skills of the game is a requirement. But along with all the practice time is a commitment to believe in the possibility that by controlling our interpretation of events and our approach to hitting a particular shot we have the opportunity to maximize our potential. Playing with confidence ultimately is not an aftereffect; it is a choice. The power lies solely with us. The key to tapping into that power resides in the questions we ask ourselves when we compete, whether it's on the PGA Tour or in our usual Saturday morning game. That's something we'll get into next.

CHAPTER 4

Fearless Golf's Guiding Questions

Frank Gasaway was a thirty-one-year-old professional golfer widely known around Atlanta as an excellent money player. Whether the match was for $50 a hole or $5,000 a hole, Frank was always up for the challenge of playing for money. As the stakes and the level of competition increased, so did the quality of Frank's play. With money on the line, he made birdies when it counted. His scores for money matches were often incredibly low. Whenever I went to a tournament, I would hear stories of how Frank birdied this or that hole to close out a match and win the kind of money that would make most of us blush and some of us break into a cold sweat. Despite his clearly demonstrated ability to consistently compete with the best pros in the state, Frank had one problem. He could not replicate that high quality of play in professional golf tournaments. He would routinely take money from the top golfers in the state, and then he wouldn't even qualify for the events that those same golfers were winning.

Practice rounds in the low to mid-60s typically and illogically were followed by competitive rounds in the mid- to high 70s. If he was ever leading a tournament, he would find a way to sabotage himself. He missed qualifying for the U.S. Open by a mere stroke because he double-bogeyed the seventeenth hole (after a bogey-free day of golf to that point). Making matters all the more interesting was that there was a time when Frank was an excellent tournament golfer: As a high schooler, Frank had once shot 28 for nine holes, then the national record.

Imagine my predicament as a psychologist facing a golfer who could play great golf when it was for money but who could not play well in tournaments. The fact that it happened consistently led me to realize that there was a definite pattern in place.

I asked Frank to take me through his routine and thought patterns as he approached a money match. He told me this: *"I warm up on the range, check how my swing feels, and just try to get loose. In the back of my mind as I'm doing this, I feel like I am going to bury whoever I am playing. I love competing against other people."*

I asked him to tell me the things he says to himself as he plays. He took me through a recent money match:

On the first tee I was thinking "Where do I want to hit the ball?" I told myself that I wanted to hit it down the right side of the fairway. Though I was thinking of hitting it down the middle, the ball ended up in the bunker. I didn't really care though because I know that I am a good bunker player. I'm thinking, "What do I need to do to beat this guy?" So I hit a nice shot out of there, saved par, and halved the hole. The next hole was a par 5. I was certain that I could reach if I kept it in play, so I hit a nice drive into a wide part of the fairway, wondering, "How far do I have to the center of the green?" I hit the shot to the front edge and two-putted for birdie. I won the hole.

I then asked Frank to take me through what he thinks as he approaches tournaments. His approach was very different.

On the drive to this last tournament I found myself thinking "What if I shoot 80 today?" [he was thinking this despite the fact that he'd shot 67, 72, 70 in his previous three rounds]. On the first tee I'm thinking, "God, let me play good enough to not embarrass myself. What if I make a fool of myself again?" In the back of my mind I'm wondering what everyone is thinking of me. I was just hoping not to put the ball into the creek. My whole body was tight, and my swing was short.

So what happened?

I managed to put that ball in the fairway, and then I was playing all right. I made a few pars but I was still tight. I wasn't feeling good. In the back of my mind I was still wondering, "What if I blow it?" Then on number 7 I just blocked this ball out to the right. I don't even know where it went, man. I had to drop next to the ladies' tee, that's how far right it was! I made triple on that hole, followed by a bogey on 8. After blocking the ball on number 7, I asked myself, "What are you doing? How can you be so stupid?"

Obviously, these sorts of questions led Frank to a rather bad place mentally, a place from where he could not recover. He followed that hole up with bogeys until he was far enough out of the lead that it didn't matter what he shot. Conversely, for money matches, Frank saw nothing but fairways. He asked good, directed questions: Where do I want to hit the ball? How far do I have to the center of the green? His mind was on hitting shots at targets on a golf course the way that mastery golfers typically do. He said,

> I am not really too focused on winning holes. I don't mind it if I go one up or one down. I am more focused on getting into my own rhythm, getting a feel for the course. It doesn't really matter what happens early on because I know that I'll have my shots down the line. I just focus on trying to hit good shots.

Tournament golf patterns were the exact opposite. Frank thought about nothing but his score. He saw nothing but the hazards, and he approached shots trying to avoid those hazards (water to the right, out-of-bounds to the left). He asked anxiety-producing questions ("What if I shoot 80 today? What if I make a fool of myself again? What are you doing? How can you be so stupid?"). He totally ignored finding his rhythm. And his perspective changed from mastery golf (playing the course) to ego golf (trying to impress others or not embarrass himself) and by asking such poor, ego-oriented questions, he created the very escalating distractions and fear that mastery golfers are immune to. For every question that leads to bad thoughts, there is an equally uncomfortable answer that produces the type of fear that ensures those bad thoughts result in bad swings.

Bad questions focused on future uncertainties or past difficulties produce a cycle of fear that feeds on itself. The way to stop that cycle is to redirect that focus with good, mastery-oriented questions. *"How am I going to win this golf tournament?"* is how Jack Nicklaus approached every event he ever entered. It is heroic in its simplicity. Its directness is the hallmark of a mastery-oriented, fearless golfer.

In literature and film, the goal of many authors and filmmakers is to use their medium as a vehicle to discover the perfect hero. I sometimes wonder what it would be like to have that sort of freedom as a psychologist, to take a golfer and mold him into the perfect model of mastery golf. Such a golfer would have aspects of Hogan, Nicklaus, Woods, certainly, but there'd be the passion of a survivor like Chris DiMarco, the innocent tenacity of a Heath Slocum or Jonathan Byrd, and the quiet resolve of David Toms, too. No doubt, he would be an interesting mix of Luke Skywalker and Peter Parker and James Bond and Harry Callahan and so many of my favorite film and book heroes growing up: unassuming, uncomplicated, and pure in their motivations.

jack's two favorite questions

Fear-filled golfers tend to ask themselves negative questions focused on future uncertainties. Questions like: What if I slice or How am I losing to him or Why can't I play well when it counts? Golfers who learn to control the questions they program into their minds are at a distinct advantage compared to those who wait passively for the situation to determine the question. Jack Nicklaus once said that he had two favorite questions that he forced himself to focus on throughout every round:

How am I going to win this golf tournament?

How do I want to play this shot?

It's natural to think of silly questions, but it's not productive to focus on these questions with uncertain negative potential. Instead, focus on the job of hitting quality shots at specific targets. Questions that focus the mind on details relevant to hitting great shots at precise targets are the key component to mastery golf.

The real world of golf, however, is different from the scripted world of novels or films. Real people are complex and motivated by various, often conflicting drives. Mastery golf is always a matter of degree, and real golfers in real life playing in front of real galleries (or real golfers simply trying to play their best in a match with their friends, coworkers, or business associates) often need help remaining focused on the things that count. As we've seen from the preceding chapters, this is what happens when fear and fear-based questions interrupt the potential for success. It is why Frank Gasaway played golf with two different personalities. It is a large part of the explanation for why you seem to play effortlessly on some rounds or even some holes, only to struggle like a beginner at other times.

But I think there is hope for a recovery and that hope is going to begin with an analysis of the questions we ask ourselves when we play. Those questions make everything possible.

For instance, recall how Davis Love III was able to shift his focus on the eighteenth hole at Pebble Beach from an ego mode to a mastery mode simply by changing his question about the status of his opponents to "What is my target?" While ego-oriented golfers are asking themselves questions that have to do with outcomes and personal emotional status (such as, "How will I look if I miss this shot?" or "How much is this shot worth?"), I have found that mastery golfers typically ask themselves the same few questions over and over again:

What is my target?
What is the best way to play this hole?

What sort of shot does this hole require?

How do I want to hit this shot?

Because the mind often returns answers in visual form to the questions we ask ourselves, it is no wonder that mastery golfers are able to stay more focused and composed. The questions they ask themselves keep them focused on hitting shots at targets, a process which negates the fear that often accompanies performing in front of a crowd.

In fact, asking questions is a core part of the self-dialogues we all conduct (what William James called "the I and the Me"). We all ask questions because asking questions helps us navigate the complex waters of our individual worlds. In our everyday lives, we can all work ourselves into hysterical panics through the questions we ask: What if I have cancer? What if my job is at risk? What if my kids are on drugs? What if I am going bald? What if I never find someone to love?

In golf, as we've seen, questions that focus on future uncertainties lead to bad mental processes. I constantly remind golfers I work with not to hide from any of the obstacles that golf throws at them. Repeat: We do not run from obstacles. Rather, we identify them, learn about them, and then figure out how to effectively overcome them. Questions focus our minds in the same way a lens focuses a laser. Questions that focus the mind on details relevant to hitting great shots at precise targets are the key component of mastery golf.

I have met literally thousands of golfers in my life, and there are as many bad questions as there are golfers. One PGA

Tour rookie asked, *"What if I don't make a cut all year? What if I can't pay my bills? What if I never make it on Tour?"* All of us average golfers too often ask ourselves *"What if I hook? What if I slice? What if I miss this putt?"* And for all the poor questions that lead to bad thoughts, there is an answer that produces the type of fear that ensures those bad thoughts result in bad swings.

As with most of life's mysteries, the solution to this common psychological ailment is simplicity. Because just as the mind instinctively responds to poor questions, it also responds instinctively to great questions like "How do I want to play this shot?" or "What is my target?" These are questions with immediate, knowable answers. Those are the questions of a golfer in control of his game and of his emotions.

bad questions vs. good questions

Here is a list of bad questions that can invade a golfer's internal conversation and short circuit his system for success. Notice how difficult they are to answer in a constructive way:

What if
 . . . I slice?
 . . . I choke?

cont. on next page

cont. from previous page

... I shoot 80 today?

... I don't make a cut all year?

... I have to go back to Qualifying School?

... I hit it into that water on 13?

... I make a fool of myself?

... I lose?

... I hook?

... I get nervous?

... I get hit by lightning?

... this shot ends up in the weeds?

... I embarrass myself, again?

Can

... I play any worse?

... I try to not embarrass myself today?

Are

... they going to think I am getting worse?

When

... did I become such a choker?

... am I going to stop embarrassing myself?

... is this nightmare going to end?

Where

... has my confidence gone?

... has my tempo gone?

cont. on next page

cont. from previous page

    . . . has my putting touch gone?

    . . . is your brain, dummy?

    . . . is this shot going to end up?

How

    . . . can I be so stupid?

    . . . could I have missed that putt?

    . . . many shots am I going to throw away today?

    . . . on earth, at this age, did I make such a stupid mistake?

    . . . am I losing to him?

    . . . bad can this round of golf get?

    . . . awful can I play?

    . . . bad am I playing today?

    . . . embarrassing can this get?

    . . . will history judge me?

Why

    . . . me?

    . . . do I even play this game?

    . . . didn't I chip out on that last hole?

    . . . are my hands shaking?

    . . . can't I ever play well when it counts?

Will

    . . . they be impressed?

cont. on next page

cont. from previous page

Who

. . . is chasing me?

. . . is the best player in the group?

Am

. . . I ever going to learn?

. . . I really this bad?

Which

. . . Mike is going to show up today?

Does

. . . coach think much of my game?

Now, here is a list of productive, directed, specific questions that are the hallmark of the successful, fearless golfer.

What is my goal for this round?
What is my strategy?
What is my target?

We prefer the shorter list. Pay attention to the questions you ask yourself. If they tend to fit in with the first section of open-ended, unanswerable, and self-destructive hypotheses, try to redirect that inquisitiveness toward a group of questions that you not only know the answer to, but that will also help move your game forward.

Interviews with PGA Tour golfers revealed that they very often use powerful questions to focus their awareness and block out distractions. And although the questions they ask are often determined by the situation they are in (for example, Jack Nicklaus asking *"How am I going to win this golf tournament?"* before his final round at the 1986 Masters), the best golfers in the world typically focus on three key questions before and during a round of competitive golf to guide their thinking and keep them focused on playing mastery golf. I call these golf's guiding questions, and you don't have to be playing for a green jacket to make them work for you.

before a round: what are my obstacles/what is my strategy today?

If you study those individuals who have been able to rise to the summit of their respective domains, what becomes clear is that the approach to success begins with a controlled attitude. Although my primary area of research and practice is golf, there is much to be learned from other competitive domains as well. I have not only studied successful businessmen such as Cornelius Vanderbilt and Henry Ford, but also great military and political strategists, scientists and artists, and legendary coaches who have paved the pathway to understanding how to help athletes perform their best. Regardless of which sport you are talking about, there are some common themes that all great coaches address in their philosophies. The ideas of confidence, optimism, hard work, perseverance, and discipline are timeless and universal across all pursuits.

Another universal aspect to success in sports, perhaps the single most important aspect that all great coaches talk about, is the importance of *preparing your mind to win*. In fact, the historically great leaders in every competitive domain have spoken at some point or other about the importance of preparing yourself for victory. We all have heard the military strategist Sun Tzu's immortal words that "all battles are won before they are ever fought," or the simple guidance offered by UCLA basketball coach John Wooden, who was fond of saying, "Failing to prepare is preparing to fail."

But what does it mean to be prepared to play great golf? Is it simply a function of believing in yourself, or feeling confident, as some would have you believe? Is simply visualizing putts going in the hole the essence of great preparation? Not necessarily. My interviews with the best golfers in the world suggested that rooted in their preparation are guiding questions that allow them to gauge how well they are swinging and putting so they know what they will and won't be capable of that day.

A key distinction between fearless and frightened golfers is the tendency to either try to ignore obstacles and adversity, and pretend they do not exist, or to identify and acknowledge those obstacles in advance, and prepare as well as possible to overcome them. Note that their questions are not about who they are playing with, what they get if they win, or how badly they want to beat their opponent. Rather, their questions focus on their games and the golf course, and how they are going to get the most out of their games to play that course as well as they can. This question often has to do with aggressive or conservative approaches; whether to aim at flags near hazards or centers of greens and try to make longer putts.

The reason it is important to ask these questions before a round of golf is because golf is, by many accounts, the most difficult game in the world. To me, that makes it also the most interesting game in the world. Golf's difficulty doesn't lie in simply hitting a golf ball; any beginner can do that. The difficulty lies in the fact that golf is so very, very sensitive to psychological and mechanical fluctuation. Even subtle changes in an individual's mood, tension levels, confidence, muscular stiffness, or swing path can result in dramatic differences in shots and in subsequent scores. Thus it requires a precision and consistency that other sports do not. And, as an added bonus, it offers plenty of time between shots to think about that difficulty. These are the obstacles that golfers face, and the obstacles that they prepare for before they play golf.

Almost by default, top golfers ask effective questions that prepare them to play their best. For instance, Jack Nicklaus would warm up on the driving range being guided by the simple question *"What are my parameters today?"* In other words, Jack wanted to know how well he was hitting the ball that day so he knew how risky or conservative he had to play. He wanted to know whether his swing was a bit loose so that, rather than attack pins, he could hit to the center of greens until he could figure it out. As he said,

> while I am warming up before a round of golf I am just trying to understand my parameters that day so if I need to, I can take away 20 percent of my game, cut the golf course in half, and limit my errors. It isn't me at my best, but a lot of times it takes bogey out of the equation, and lets me survive until I can work it out on the range afterward.

Tiger Woods's pregame preparation is similar. Tiger is always guided by the philosophy to "prepare for the worst, but expect the best." Tiger knows that we all go through daily fluctuations. We are just a bit different from one day to the next; some days we are tighter or stiffer, or our tempo may be a bit quicker, or we are perhaps not seeing the greens the same way we did the day before.

On that point great champions are consistent: Because there is daily fluctuation built into the human condition, their goal is to understand themselves to the degree that they know what they are able to do on a given day.

Indeed, self-knowledge and self-understanding are what allow Tiger to know whether he has to play with his A, B, or C game. Thus, asking questions rooted in managing your games before a round of golf is the first key to effectively preparing to win golf tournaments.

matt kuchar: scoring blind

Recall that Matt Kuchar won his first pro tournament, the 2002 Honda Classic, by shooting 66 in the final round. Of the round, he said,

> I didn't really look at what scores the leaders shot, how many back I was. I went out there to the first tee, hit the first tee shot. I didn't look at a leaderboard and didn't know how I stood. And today, I didn't look at a leaderboard until 17, and I actually . . . I got in the scorer's tent and I'm adding up my scores, and, of course, you go hole-by-hole. And I add up my scores, compared to what the scorecard says on each 9, and I see I shoot a 35 on the front. And I add up the back nine on the little marker's scores of my notes, and I see, 1-under, 2-under, 3-under, 4-under, 5-under? Is that right? Some good memories were brought back, talking some golf psychology earlier this week. He said, "Matt just put your head down. Don't worry about where you stand. Don't worry about how somebody else stands. Go play golf, add it up at the end, and if you win, that's great."

on the tee box: what is the best strategy for this hole?

As various books on golf psychology point out, two of the most common problems that golfers face are getting too far ahead of themselves by thinking of outcomes, and dwelling on the past by thinking of what has happened on previous holes. In other words, one of the biggest challenges that golfers face is *staying in the present*. As it usually happens, bad holes carry over to create more bad holes. Bad putts on previous greens translate into bad drives on subsequent tees, and oftentimes golfers are so wrapped up in a previous hole that their mind is not focused on how best to play the current hole.

As I have explained, even golfers who know that they need to stay in the present don't necessarily know *how* to stay in the present. The solution is not to simply tell yourself to stay in the present. Telling yourself to stay in the present is like telling yourself "Don't worry" when trying to give a speech in front of your peers. Telling yourself not to worry usually means that you are worrying, and that is likely to create more worry. Telling yourself to stay in the present usually means you aren't in the present. There has to be a better way.

That better way is to do the things you naturally do at those times when staying in the present is easy. When golf is easy, golfers ask themselves the right questions automatically. They don't have to think about asking themselves natural questions like "How do I want to play this hole" or "How do I want to play this shot?" They just do it. They do not need to remind themselves to stay in the present because they *are* in the present, asking questions that focus their mind on hitting shots around a golf course.

---

words of a champion: raymond floyd

What would make you think Raymond Floyd would win the 1986 U.S. Open at Shinnecock Hills? At one point in the final round he was only one of the eight players tied for the lead in the championship. And of those tied for the lead, he was the only one who had blown a comfortable final round lead the week before. He also was the only one nearly forty-four years old, which was too old to win the U.S. Open. And he was the only one who had won just one tournament in the previous four years.

But Floyd was always one of the game's great competitors. He learned a bit about himself in losing that lead the previous week, and he took some time to learn a great deal about how to play Shinnecock in the days leading to the championship.

That self-awareness, that commitment, that resolve is what defines a champion in an eight-man tie in the final round of a major. Floyd's words that day reflect that sense of confidence at the moment of truth.

cont. on next page

cont. from previous page

"I was in total control," he said.

I was never fast with any swing, which is phenomenal for me. I was walking at a speed in sync with my golf swing. I felt together. I was never upset, and I never let anything bother me. I stuck to my game plan and didn't deviate.

I decided I wasn't going to deviate, no matter what. Believe me, every player looks at the scoreboard. You can't miss it. I wish I didn't have to look at it. It can make you change your plan. But today I never deviated.

Thursday, we played in terrible weather, and that was as trying as shooting the blowout round. The thing was I continued to do my best and tell myself, "Don't deviate." I guarantee you I won the tournament on Thursday.

I pride myself on being able to handle the pressure and control myself mentally. I've been known as a frontrunner. When you're in front, I know you have to live with the emotions of leading. I know emotions. That's what separates you on tour. Last week, I totally blew it internally. My wife, Maria, and I discussed it on the long ride out here Sunday night. At first I didn't feel like discussing it, but you have to go back sometimes and counter a bad situation and make it into a positive learning experience.

As part of their routine, on each and every tee box, mastery golfers incorporate into their routine the question, "What is the best strategy for this hole?" If the mind automatically responds to internal questions, then a simple, "What is the best strategy for this hole?" is a great way to bring golfers into the present by staving off questions that lock them into the past or get them too far into the future. Think of it like a gavel coming down and bringing a meeting to order: The time for useless chatter is done; it is time now to get down to business. It gets them refocused on the golf course and playing mastery golf.

at address: what is my target?

Thinking about obstacles is fine before a round of golf because it fosters preparedness and guards golfers against the surprises that often lead to panic and fear. But one does not want to be thinking about obstacles right before or during a golf swing. Similarly, thinking about strategy for playing a particular hole is important on the tee box because it allows golfers to minimize the chances of getting into trouble. Hole strategy gives them a better chance of hitting the right clubs at the right time. But still, when preparing to hit a golf shot, golfers do not want to be thinking of strategy. Rather, they want their minds exclusively focused on making a fearless swing at a precise and specific target.

The key question that brings golfers into the moment and

gives them the best chance at making fearless swings at specific targets is to ask themselves before each and every shot, "What is my target?" When golfers ask themselves this question, their mind simply reacts. It focuses on a target in the distance. Once golfers are able to lock on to specific targets, they are then better able to trust their golf swings and simply hit to the target. When golfers are focused on targets, it means that they are not focused on swing mechanics, not focused on outcomes, and not focused on the past, future, or other golfers. Being in the present fosters asking the question "What's my target?" Asking that question brings golfers into the present.

Confidence Drill: Your New Mantra

For those looking to further instill the principles of mastery golf in their games, the words "What's my target?" need to reach the stage of a mantra. In Hinduism and Buddhism, a mantra is defined as a sacred verbal formula repeated in prayer or meditation. It is believed that when vocalized and focused the mantra has the power to become a reality. There is no more beneficial reality than keeping "What's my target?" first and foremost in your mind.

When golfers don't actively put good questions into their heads, oftentimes either the situation or random stream of consciousness thinking puts negative questions there. Standing over an important shot, imagine the difference between asking yourself, "What is the leader doing now?" or asking, "What's my target?" Think of the difference between asking, "How did I bogey the last hole?" and asking, "What's my target?" Think of the difference between asking, "What if I leave another drive out to the right?" and asking, "What's my target?"

Those other questions may exist in your mind, but always returning to the mastery golfer's mantra—"What's my target?"—will improve your focus and most likely your chance for success.

Asking "What's my target" brings the mind into focus, and lets golfers' natural instincts take over. Simply focusing on that question often brings golfers into the present, and allows them to control the moment. "What's my target?" is the greatest question in golf, and a golfer's greatest mental weapon against falling prey to nervous situations. As golf professional Nick Cassini explained:

> When I ask the question "What's my target?" it is like everything else goes away. I am able to see where I want the ball to go. And the smaller the target the better because even if I miss the target, I am still in the fairway or on the green. It's amazing, really, how such a simple question can mean so much in a round of golf. So now whenever I find myself not concentrating, or wondering about outcomes or thinking about work, I simply ask myself, "What's my target" and focus on that target. I can't believe what a difference that makes, really!

At its best, golf is a game of simply hitting shots to targets. That's it. That's all. At its best, a golfer's quiet mind goes something like this:

1. "What's my target?"
2. A specific target in the distance is picked out.
3. The target is locked on to with 100 percent concentration.
4. A fearless golf swing is made at that target.

Pretty boring. But here's a newsflash: Boring works. Because just about every shot in golf—from drives, to long irons, to short irons, and even to chipping and putting—boils down to hitting the ball at a specific target, "What is my target?" is the great question in all of golf, and is often a mastery golfer's greatest weapon against the negative thoughts that can creep in and create fear. "What is my target?" is the trigger that allows him to make fearless swings at precise targets.

words of a champion: retief goosen

How many things does a champion have to overcome? In winning the 2004 U.S. Open, Retief Goosen played a difficult course set up to an almost absurd level of difficulty. With the greens at Shinnecock Hills baked and hard and

cont. on next page

cont. from previous page

fast, Goosen putted his way to a victory. But it was not merely the course, Goosen had to overcome a partisan crowd desperately rooting Phil Mickelson toward a comeback victory. Mickelson played valiantly down the stretch, but Goosen withstood it. Goosen battled bad swings and bad lies, but his putter would not let him down. He one-putted 11 greens in the final round, including seven straight times in the final seven holes. How could he do that under such conditions? His answer to the media afterward was simple and direct, just as you'd expect from a fearless golfer committed to playing the golf course, not the circumstances. To win, to be successful, these are the things that are required.

When you stand over a putt you are nervous. You are shaking on the inside like any other player does, and Tiger does, too. It's just how you've learned to play under that sort of pressure, and in a way it sort of becomes natural in a way that you feel like I can only play my best golf when I'm really under pressure.

Sometimes when you're not under pressure, your focus is not there, and you might not make the putts. But when you're sort of under pressure, it's a must thing; you must focus and you must make the putt, and that's what I feel when I stand over it.

CHAPTER 5

The Attributions
that Golfers Make

Battles are won before they are fought.

—Sun Tzu

I recall a memorable phone call I received a couple of years ago from a professional golfer with whom I had worked named John Orrell. John had a strong ego orientation (see Chapter 2) when he first came to me, and our time together had been spent working on how to best prepare him and his mind to focus on the golf course rather than on other golfers. To play better, John had to learn to focus properly, and to focus properly John had to commit to understanding the golf course and keeping that concern foremost in his mind, eliminating all other thoughts. By knowing the course and knowing his ideal targets in advance, John was able to better ignore other players and leaderboards. It was his best way to prepare for tournament golf. Soon after he adopted this strategy, John began to experience success.

On the day of this particular phone call, however, John had had an awful round, shooting his highest score in a competitive tournament in five years.

"Why do you think you played so badly, John?" I asked, attempting to get at how he was thinking after the round. In other words, I was asking, "To what do you attribute such a bad round of golf?" Psychologists use the term *attributions* to describe the reasons that people provide for their successes and failures in the things they attempt. It's this kind of post-round talk that reveals great things about how strong our sense of self-efficacy is and whether we have adopted a mastery approach to the game so we are more likely to play fearless golf.

John's response to my question was initially not ideal. He began telling me hole by hole about the shots he had hit. He told me of errant drives, mishit irons, and missed putts. He told me about incorrect distances and wrong clubs as well as about his futile attempt to quiet his mind. At one point he questioned whether he really had the ability to compete at that level. (Do you see a pattern here?) In all, he told me that the reason he had played badly was a combination of mechanical and equipment factors. The ironic thing is that he had shot 67 the day before at a more difficult course with those very same mechanics and the very same clubs.

After he finished pouring his heart out, I sat quietly, letting the weight of the silence work on him.

"Are you there?" he asked after a moment.

"I'm here," I replied.

"Well . . . what do you think, Doc?" he inquired.

I repeated to him the most foundational phrase I use with golfers. "John," I said, "I think that battles are won before they are ever fought."

He didn't respond at first, but then he said, "But I've been working hard on my swing and on picking targets and being fearless like we worked on." His voice gave him away.

"What did you do in your practice rounds before the tournament?" I asked, knowing the answer.

"I didn't play a practice round."

I said nothing, waiting for him to finish my unspoken thought. "I know what you are going to say: I didn't know the course and the yardage, and that caused me to hesitate and to be indecisive in my golf swing. And I know you can't play good golf being indecisive."

I corrected him. "No, you cannot play good competitive golf being indecisive. You can accidentally hit shots with good results. But playing well by accident is not how you want to attempt to groove success. You want to establish a method and an approach that fuel success, that set you up to succeed. To play your best, and especially to play well in a competitive atmosphere, being decisive and having a plan are crucial."

He admitted as much. "My hesitation and indecision caused me to miss a couple of shots early, which made me more tentative. So my poor play is really rooted in the fact that I didn't prepare."

"So when," I asked, "did you really blow this tournament? Rethink what you said earlier, and tell me why you played badly."

"I blew it the week before the tournament," he replied, "because battles are won before they are fought. I played badly because I was unsure about the course . . . and that was because I didn't play a practice round the day before. I didn't prepare to play the golf course and my old, bad habits came back."

After first providing reasons that had little to do with his lack of success, John finally was able to identify the proper attribution. That kind of unqualified self-assessment is what we should strive for. Anything less than the brutal truth holds us back from the possibility of our potential.

Let's be clear: Making it possible to play your best golf—whether you're trying to win a major championship, earn your Tour card, or shoot a personal best on your home course, is not just about the right amount of physical and mental preparation prior to your round. It isn't just how you approach the round, and it isn't just about the way you control your mind and focus during the round. Although often overlooked, how you reflect on a performance (the attributions you make about your play) determines how you can improve.

As a psychologist, one of my favorite professional and personal activities is listening to the reasons individuals give for their successes and failures. All day, every day, at work and at play, whether watching others or watching themselves, people inevitably give reasons for "why" things happen. Before beginning this chapter, I went into the files I keep on the golfers I've spoken with and made a list of some of the causes to which golfers attribute their success and failure. I call it my "Because" file and here are some of the more memorable self-assessments. No doubt you may recognize some of these as having been your own on occasion.

BECAUSE . . .

It's a Fazio course. I always play well on Fazio
   courses.

I have no confidence in my game.

My alignment is off.

My hands are not setting properly at the top.

I'm working with a new instructor.

I'm too small.

I'm too heavy.

My weight is too much on the outside of my knees instead of the inside.

My eyes are behind the line.

I'm very flexible.

My eyes are over the line.

My grip is too weak.

My grip is too strong.

I lose my focus and concentration.

I started late in golf.

I get too caught up in what other players in my group
   are doing.

Yellow balls don't travel as far as white balls.

This shirt is unlucky.

My temper gets the best of me.

I could smell the cigarette smoke of someone on another hole.

I hit the ball too low to score here.

I don't hit the ball long enough to score here.

I'm too old (the game has passed me).

I'm too young (no experience).

It's cold.

It's windy.

The greens are bad.

It was a difficult course.

My preparation from last week carried over.

My father never gave me approval.

I haven't played in a long time.

I play too much.

I don't play enough.

I didn't get to warm up.

I warmed up too long, got tired on the range.

The 14th hole got me.

I have poor self-esteem.

I couldn't get into the flow.

I don't know.

I was thinking where I don't want to hit it rather than where I do want to hit it.

This course doesn't set up well for me.

I don't like who I was paired with.

I felt tight all day.

My brother got all the attention growing up.

I play too much (fatigue).

I play too little (rusty).

I argued with my wife and that was on my mind.

I'm too stressed.

There's a flinch in my swing.

The courses I play are fairly wet.

My swing is off plane.

My preshot routine stinks.

I found a new waggle.

I stand too close.

I am sliding my hips.

I bought a new driver.

I am past parallel.

I am getting started inside.

I never move my right knee.

I was focused on what I wanted to do with the ball.

I misread the greens.

My hands are too high.

I am using a new putter.

I have great hands.

Attributions are psychologically interesting because they are based on perceived—rather than actual—causes. They are immensely important because inaccurate attributions are often the critical element that instigate and sustain the ruts that golfers fall into. In addition, they often constitute that monumentally thin line that separates bad golfers from good golfers, and good golfers from great golfers. If you are a good golfer stuck at a plateau, or a golfer whose progress in the game has been more sideways than forward, then you will want to read closely. A better understanding of psychological attributions may well be the key to unlocking your golfing potential.

heath slocum and the power of framing

Heath Slocum serves as a model of effective thinking. In 2000 he shot 81 in the final day of Qualifying School to miss having an exemption on the PGA Tour by a single stroke. The failure meant that he would be forced to compete on a less prestigious, less competitive tour for another year. His dream of playing on the PGA Tour would have to wait, and there was no guarantee that he would have this type of opportunity again. After being a first team All-American in college, Heath saw himself and his position in golf as a failure. Heath was dejected, gloomy, downhearted, and spiritless, but his father was finally able to help him frame the situation and turn the negative into a positive. Heath's father, whom Heath describes as "one of the most positive people I know," told him,

> Heath, you can either look at this as a *failure*, or as an *opportunity*. Do you realize how close you are

cont. on next page

cont. from previous page
to getting on the PGA Tour? In order to get on the PGA Tour, all you have to do is finish in the top fifteen on this Tour, and you'll be playing on the PGA Tour next year. You shouldn't be disappointed for what you haven't done, but excited for what you have done, and can do in the future.

This advice helped Heath frame his experience differently. He saw opportunity where before he had seen only failure and disappointment. He felt energized where before he'd only felt drained. His hunger returned and midway through that season, Heath had won three times on the BUY.COM Tour and had earned a spot on the PGA Tour for the following year.

the power of "because"

Poet Alexander Pope once said that "to err is human." One of the most consistently human errors is the tendency for people to attribute success and failure to perceived rather than actual causes. For example, it is quite common for schoolkids to say things like "I failed the test because the teacher hates me" or "I failed the test because Miss Crabapple is mean." In reality, it is usually far more likely that the actual reason they failed was simply because they didn't study correctly or prepare properly.

The problem with misattributions is not simply that they are an inaccurate reflection of reality. Misattributing our failures—and our successes—has powerful consequences for subsequent behavior and corrective action. Students who believe they failed a test because the teacher doesn't like them may try to get on a teacher's good side, believing that this will bring them better test scores. From my personal experience as a teacher, let me assure you that this strategy is unlikely to succeed. What those students probably won't do is correct their faulty study habits, the actual cause of their poor performance. Unfortunately, it is often just such misattributions that launch the cycle of academic failure for many students.

On the other hand, students who believe that their poor test scores are rooted in poor study habits (regardless of their feelings about their teacher) are more likely to spend some time trying to develop better study habits. This is certainly more likely to produce better test scores down the road than relying on the good graces of a buttered-up teacher. The important point is that the steps that students take toward trying to improve are directly determined by the reasons they "believe" they failed in the first place.

Golfers make attributions about everything from why their drives fade to the right (my feet are too close to the ball) to why they miss putts (this putter has no feel) to why they invariably underhit shots from the sandtrap (my club is allergic to sand). Interesting to me as a psychologist is how much time golfers spend practicing to get better but how little time they spend trying to make accurate attributions to ensure that what they are practicing is the right thing for the right reasons. Woe to the golfer who focuses on a grip change to fix a slice, when the real culprit is poor alignment.

Similarly, golfers who attribute bad shots to poor mechanics rather than to grip pressure may try to make unnecessary, and ultimately unsuccessful, changes in their swings. Golfers who believe that their poor play is the result of poor equipment often spend a good deal of cash purchasing equipment and then long months adapting to it. Sometimes their attributions are correct. After all, new equipment can, and often does, make marked improvements in one's game. But for golfers whose actual shortcomings are rooted in swing flaws or unproductive thinking, new equipment is as unlikely to improve their game as a new pen is to improve a writer's prose. In both cases, the underlying causes for the poor results are rooted in poor habits or poor thinking, not poor equipment.

Fearless Golf and the Dreaded Four-Footer

Putting can be the most insidious source of frustration in the game. A lack of success on the greens easily creeps into every aspect of a player's game all the way back to the tee box. And it can fundamentally undermine the self-efficacy all golfers need if they're going to maximize their potential. But how you respond to a stretch of less than successful putting is more the problem than any physical flaw. Since putting problems can easily have an overstated effect on scoring, it is not unusual for a golfer to begin to think he is scoring badly when he is putting badly, and it is not too far from that point that a sense of putting badly leads a player to believe he is playing badly.

The mind comes back with a response something to the effect of, "I am scoring badly because I am not making enough putts, and I am not making enough putts because I can't feel the ball coming off this putter." In the fraction of an instant it takes the mind to process those thoughts, a golfer has made a more important decision than he or she may even know. After all, the golfer has just attributed poor putting performance to the putter, an equipment attribution. The solution for this is usually to go out and try new putters until one is found that feels just right. Quite naturally, golfers who make equipment attributions involving their putters will switch to a putter with which they feel comfortable in the belief, alas, that this will be the ultimate solution to their putting problem.

But let's go back for a minute. Let's say that in this case, the actual reason this particular golfer was putting badly was because his setup was off (which is the single most common reason why good golfers stop making putts). In short, focusing on the putter as the source of frustration is like believing you were caught speeding because your car is red. Truth is, painting your car white won't deter a patrolman from pulling you over if you're going eighty-five miles per hour. What's the real reason you're not holing putts? Misplaced blame can cause a player months of frustration because though he now has a new putter, he putts with the same poor setup he had before he changed putters. Because poor alignment invariably gets worse, he will soon be putting badly with the new putter.

The downward spiral continues. In time this golfer will become frustrated and lose his patience and his confidence in his putting, a trend which will bleed into the rest of his game. This is usually about the time that golfers will call me. When I ask why they believe they are playing badly, they will answer, "Because I have no confidence." What's worse, they are completely baffled as to how, when, or why they lost their confidence, where it went, or how to get it back. What they do know is that they desperately need it.

Almost always, their loss of confidence (self-efficacy) was the *result* of poor play before it was the *cause* of poor play. Just as confidence is first a *producer* and then a *product* of great golf, lack of confidence is first a product and then a producer of poor play. After all, their low self-efficacy was justified—they aren't making any putts with their current approach. They first believed their poor putting was the result of their equipment. It was, in fact, probably a function of a personal factor, such as being misaligned. Their belief that the putter was the source of their difficulties caused them to fix something that wasn't broken—the putter. From that moment, they began their trek down a slippery slope. They continued to miss putts, which ate away at their self-efficacy. Once golfers lose their self-efficacy, their swing begins to change. Grip pressure increases, the backswing shortens, head and eyes tend to "flinch" just before impact, trying to see the result because they are so unsure of themselves. Focusing on their equipment as the source of the problem made them change putters, made lining up incorrectly a "habit," and altered their putting stroke from smooth and decisive to short, quick, and uncertain.

Clearly, these golfers do not need a new putter. In many cases they merely needed to move their foot back an inch and get their eyes over the ball. As the old saying goes, "An ounce of prevention is worth a pound of cure." The more that golfers can make accurate attributions, the less time they spend climbing out of holes they themselves dig.

Attribution at its worst is the sort of Monday-morning quarterbacking that makes for good sports talk radio but rarely does anything constructive. More likely, it corrupts or destroys our confidence. However, attribution at its best is the sort of powerful education that lies at the foundation of a commitment to improve.

The Attribution Tripod

The attributions for success and failure that golfers make typically fall into three key categories. The key to consistent improvement is to accurately identify which of the following factors are responsible for your golfing performance.

1. **Personal/physical factors** include individual health and fitness issues as well as swing mechanics and things such as grip, alignment, ball position, grip pressure, hip and shoulder turns.

2. **Psychological factors** include attributions, achievement orientations, self-efficacy, anxiety, trusting your swing, and the other ideas covered in this book.

3. **Equipment** includes drivers, fairway woods, putters, irons, wedges, and the golf ball, maybe even shoes, socks, hat, and glove, depending on how much uncertainty has invaded a golfer's mind.

One of the patterns that is important is the amount of control golfers feel they have over the things that influence their games. Indeed, because control is the foundation of our confidence, *believing we can control the things that influence our golf* is essential to playing with confidence.

words of a champion: jack nicklaus

In 1980, Jack Nicklaus was coming off his worst year as a pro, and his detractors were predicting that his time as a dominant player might be over. But Nicklaus, at age forty, still had the desire to be great, especially at the greatest events. In 1980, he won both the U.S. Open, setting a scoring record, and the PGA Championship, by a record-setting seven-stroke margin. It prompted one scoreboard

cont. on next page

cont. from previous page

operator at the U.S. Open at Baltusrol to post the phrase "Jack Is Back" next to Nicklaus's winning score.

How did the greatest player in the history of the game come back? Well, what's interesting is that even the great ones fight fear and even the great ones need to be reenergized. Nicklaus explained those developments in a 1980 article he wrote for *Golf Digest*:

> It begins with missing the short putts—the four- and five- and six-footers you've mostly made when it mattered. Pretty soon you begin to fear leaving yourself a long putt or a chip shot, which in turn puts heavy pressure on your iron play. Then, because you feel you have to hit every approach shot stone dead, you become afraid of missing fairways, and pretty soon you're playing scared on every shot, and you *are* missing fairways *and* greens, and pitch shots and chips and the short putts become even more important. . . . And the noose keeps tightening until eventually all your confidence is gone and you've completely lost the knack of scoring. It happened to me the last two years.
>
> It gradually ate into the rest of my game until finally I suspected every element of it, when really the only serious problem was my putting stroke.

Nicklaus went on to explain the work he did to improve his game, but then he also explained something more es-

cont. on next page

cont. from previous page

sential. It shows that Nicklaus was the prototypical *kaizen* golfer, striving for continual self-improvement, despite not seeing immediate results. His potentially disastrous 1979 was a learning experience and a confirmation of his decision to play less and still excel. He set his goals and would not be deterred. He committed to an extensive evaluation of every aspect of his game, focusing particularly on his putting stroke. Similar to the way Nicklaus always played a round of golf, he had a game plan and he would not be deterred from it.

"When we arrived in Baltusrol for the Open, I felt truly confident about every element of my game for the first time in at least two years," he said. Mentally, the change in attitude was even more decisive.

I came to a conclusion that I could only be true to golf and the all the people and institutions in it if I were first true to myself. I expected excellence of myself, and golf had come to expect—and deserved—excellence of me. Therefore, I should not play unless I could give my absolute best.

I made two mistakes in 1979, but the number of tournaments I played wasn't one of them. The first and certainly worst mistake was, to put it bluntly, complacency. I assumed I could go on living on my talent without really working on my game. . . . Mistake No. 2 came when with the big

cont. on next page

cont. from previous page

cut in tournaments came a cut in practice and playing time of almost half.

I know now for sure that if I want to keep my place in golf it will take ongoing work as well as talent.

If the greatest player of all time recognizes that ongoing work is required just to keep his place in the game and to overcome the fear born out of inconsistency, isn't there something to be said for the importance of silencing our own fears through meaningful practice? You can't hope to play your best if you don't do the work. Even the most talented player ever admits as much.

While golfers may not have much control over how well they are striking the ball on any given day, they have reasonable control over how they prepare for a tournament. A key pattern among great professionals is that they allow their confidence to be grounded in things over which they have control (themselves, preparation, effort) rather than things over which they have no control (other players, course conditions, weather conditions, slow play). Similarly, top players are careful to attribute their success on the back end to these same controllable things.

the psychology of attributions

In 2003, Davis Love III had won three tournaments by the end of April. After winning the Players Championship at TPC Sawgrass with a closing round 64, he attributed his success to a number of things. Davis explained, "I am now chasing my own potential. Rather than chasing Greg Norman or Tiger, I am chasing my own potential." In addition to attributing his success to better mental preparation, he also explained how a visit with Scotty Cameron had resulted in a new putter. Davis attributed his success to mechanical and psychological improvements.

Over the years, tour players have attributed their wins and losses to a variety of things, but in the majority of cases of golfers at the highest level, the way they evaluate and examine past performances directly—and positively—impacts their future performances. Whether it's recognizing that an equipment change was an important missing piece of the puzzle, or a need to refocus on lag putting or a recognition that they did not have enough experience to deal with the emotions, what's consistent in these attributions is a commitment to moving forward while being educated by the past.

The question thus becomes, What are good attributions? Since attributions are based on beliefs, they won't always be accurate. People fall into definite attributional patterns, so what do I look for as a psychologist? I look for those things that psychologists have identified as patterns of adaptive attributions that are characteristic of successful people.

When listening to the attributions that golfers make, psychologists first look for the *accuracy* of the attribution. When a golfer says he played badly because he had no confidence, it is essential to discover whether that is the actual reason why he played badly. It is usually difficult to narrow down a single cause of golfing performance. Just as important as accurate attributions are the patterns that golfers tend to fall into when talking about golf.

In general, attributions for success and failure have three characteristics:

1. **Stability.** The causes of outcomes are stable (fixed over time) or unstable (variable over time).
2. **Locus.** The causes of outcomes are internal (due to the individual) or external (due to factors outside the individual).
3. **Controllability.** The causes of outcomes are controllable or uncontrollable.

These attributional characteristics are important to golfers. Research suggests that athletes who have a tendency to attribute their performance to *controllable* factors (effort, preparation, mental and physical skills, etc.) rather than to *uncontrollable* factors (luck, weather, etc.) typically perform better in the long run. In the example at the start of this chapter, recall John Ottrell's attributions for a poor round. "Maybe I don't have the ability to play at this level," John ultimately suggested. He was telling me that his poor play resulted from internal ("*I* can't do it") and stable (unlike effort, ability is permanent) factors that he could not control (ability is inborn). He found this most unsettling. I was able to help him see that a better and more accurate attribution was the likely cause of his problem: his preparation. Note that preparation is also internal (*I* prepare), but it can vary over time and is indeed controllable. The more that golfers can accurately attribute their performances to factors over which they have control, the better chance they have of maintaining their confidence, and ultimately building on it.

On a related note, an important pattern for golfers is how they view the notion of "ability." Psychologists have found that most people have either a *fixed* or *incremental* view of ability. Golfers like John, who see their ability as fixed, believe that they have been born with a certain amount of talent and that amount cannot be increased or decreased significantly. As you may have guessed, such golfers tend to make stable, uncontrollable attributions that serve to undermine their own confidence. After all, if natural ability is an "inborn" thing, then one is born either with it or without it.

Research in psychology suggests that people who tend to attribute their success to natural, inborn talent are similarly likely to attribute the success of other golfers to talent. When failure and success are viewed in terms of inborn talent or natural ability, factors such as preparation and hard work are not considered essential to improving one's game. People who view natural ability as the cause of success and failure are likely to explain their own failure by muttering something like, "I lost because so and so is simply *better* than I am." This reminds me of what a famous sportswriter said of Jack Nicklaus at his dominant best. Nicklaus came to be such a force over time because he intimidated his opponents, got into their heads, but he didn't really do it in an overt way. Instead, it was internalized, and as a result, probably that much more effective. As the saying went, not only did Nicklaus know he was better than all the other players, but they all knew Nicklaus was better than they were, and not only that, they all knew that Nicklaus knew he was better than they were. So Nicklaus knew if he hung around near the top of the leaderboards, eventually the others would crack before he did.

Remember how many professional golfers in the year 2000 believed that, no matter how much they practiced or improved, they simply could never expect to possess the natural skills that Tiger Woods was born with? It's certainly easy to understand the built-in edge this notion gives golfers such as Tiger or Jack. It bears asking, of course, why, if golfers such as Tiger and Jack have such natural, inborn ability, they are nearly always the ones who put forth the greatest effort, practice for longer hours than their competitors, and work to develop hardy attitudes that buttress their game. Is it possible that, at least to a great degree, the harder they work the more talented they become?

Conversely, golfers who believe that ability is incremental, or "changeable," view talent as something that is invariably tied to the amount of effort they expend. Indeed, these are precisely the golfers who believe that the harder they work the more talented they become. Such golfers tend to make internal and controllable attributions, and they respond to adversity with greater effort, persistence, and better preparation.

On this point, television host Peter Kessler once asked Jack Nicklaus if he was born a great golfer, to which Jack replied, "I don't think anyone is born a great golfer. All great golfers, all people who are truly great at anything, are not born great. They become great through desire and hard work." Similarly, Jack attributes Tiger's greatness, not to inborn uncontrollable factors, but rather to the fact that "Tiger has got a desire to win, a good work ethic, and he's a smart young man."

All good teachers know that it is important to foster in their students the belief that talent and ability are changeable, controllable aspects of development. Instead of praising students for their ability, good teachers praise effort, perseverance, and persistence as ways to overcome obstacles. It bears repeating that praising young golfers with statements such as "You are such a natural!" or "You have tremendous talent!" can often have the opposite effect intended. Praising for ability or talent tells the novice that success is a matter of natural ability (which the youngster believes one either has or does not have). How can a young golfer develop confidence in an ability she believes is beyond her control? When he fails, what can a youngster do to correct what he believes is a natural, in-born talent?

Praising for *effort* with feedback such as "You fought hard that round" or "Way to hang in there!" tells the golfer that the harder you work the more you accomplish and the more talented you become. Rather than praising for ability, great golf instructors always make it a habit to praise the effort, preparation, and persistence that it takes for a golfer to succeed.

Moreover, young golfers who come to believe that their success is the result of natural ability will surely have their self-confidence shaken once they encounter what they believe to be "more talented" golfers. If a golfer comes to believe that his ability will carry him through, when it does not he is simply left believing he just doesn't have what it takes. Conversely, young golfers who are consistently told that their golfing performance is tied to controllable factors such as effort, practice, and preparation, and who hold an incremental view of ability (that is, they have as much ability as they are willing to work for) tend to respond far better to adversity and to retain their confidence through difficult and trying times. And think for a moment: Who can ever assess a golfer's real talent with complete accuracy? Athletes surprise themselves all the time with performances that exceed even their own expectations. Talent, like commitment and heart, often lies dormant and hidden for relatively long periods of time.

For average golfers whose personal development in the game isn't measured by how much money they make playing golf with respect to other players, the challenge to keep attributions controllable might appear to be easier, but it is not. How often do we blame a bad round on a balky driver, when what may have happened was we compounded the error of a misplaced drive with poor decision-making time after time. That's why getting in the exercise of honestly evaluating a round quickly after the fact may get our attention directed to the real areas of our game that need emphasis. Moreover, it is just as helpful and perhaps even more important to our development of confidence to talk about and review the holes we played well, as it is to critically dissect the holes where we didn't score. The challenge of playing fearless golf begins with a commitment to learn from the past by thinking and talking about it productively.

typical golfing attributions

Have a look at some of the typical attributions that golfers make, as well as the characteristics that they represent. Think about where they are focused (internal/external), how they occur (stable/unstable), and their relative power (controllable/uncontrollable). The key to the power of attributions is learning to read between the lines.

LUCK: "I played well because I got a few lucky bounces." . . . "I just had horrible luck that round."

This attribution is *external*, *unstable*, *uncontrollable*, perhaps the worst kind. If we talked this way about how we played all the time we might soon give up the game.

LONG-TERM EFFORT: "I played well because I always work hard." . . . "I played poorly because I am lazy."

This is an *internal*, *stable*, *controllable* attribution. This is honest, you can choose to act on this, and you can take control of it because it is not going to vary wildly.

ABILITY: "I played well because I have natural talent." . . . "I don't have the natural talent to get much better."

This is an *internal*, *stable*, *uncontrollable* attribution. As we've seen, the first two are effective assessments. The last one, however, overtakes the others. It is self-limiting and ultimately self-defeating.

TASK DIFFICULTY: "I played well because the course was easy." . . . "This is an impossible course, poorly laid out."

Here we have *external*, *unstable*, *uncontrollable* characterizations, a veritable attribution minefield. The more you think about it, saying how we play depends on something outside of ourselves, something that changes all the time, and something we have no ownership of is very nearly pure despair.

HELP FROM OTHERS: "I am playing well because I am working with an excellent instructor." . . . "I can't find the right instructor to help me improve."

This is an *external, unstable, controllable* assessment. The latter is key. Belief in your preparation not only gives you confidence coming into a round, but it also gives you the motivation to continue with the program. Of course, your teacher could move away tomorrow, and then where would you be? The challenge is to go beyond this faith in a teacher, so that you then believe in a commitment to the process of improvement and a commitment not to the teacher, but to what he or she is teaching you.

MOOD: "I play well when I feel good." . . . "I can't seem to find my game when I'm in a lousy mood."

This is an *internal, unstable, uncontrollable* attribution. If you let your mood determine how you will play, you have forfeited control for your round. I'm not denying mood can clearly affect us. But in terms of executing positive swings at precise targets, your concentration, confidence, and self-efficacy have to exist independent of your mood. When you "can't find your game," you have to think about what your game should be. It should be focusing on the target, regardless of the circumstances. It's what successful players have learned to build into their games so that whatever their mood, they can overcome it.

how pga tour golfers talk about attributions

In the chapter on self-efficacy I explained how confidence is often rooted in the exercise of personal control. The more we believe we have control over events, the more confidence we have in our ability to achieve our goals. Indeed, whether it is to make it to the PGA Tour or to enjoy their recreational golf, golfers have developed coping habits that allow them to protect their confidence from the constant barrage of negativity, self-doubt, difficulty, and adversity built into golf. Certainly, most of that has to do with the way golfers frame their challenges, how they interpret praise and criticism, and how they deal with physiological arousal. Another reason that successful golfers are able to maintain their confidence in the face of failure and setbacks has to do with the attributions they make, specifically with the way they think of controllable versus uncontrollable attributions.

fatal attribution: mike weir

In 2003, Mike Weir turned his golfing career around. After a dismal 2002 season, he came out in 2003 and had won

cont. on next page

cont. from previous page
three times before the end of April, including his first major championship, the 2003 Masters. To what did he attribute his newfound success? Although he could have attributed it to hard work, to new equipment, to luck, or to destiny, Mike simply attributed his new success to a new attitude. He said,

> Getting ready for this year, I got away from the game for a couple of months and just needed to reassess my passion for the game and why I was playing. I was beating myself up out there, and I am not doing that anymore. I am having more fun with my golf, which allows me to relax and freewheel it a little more. The results have been terrific.

Golf is a game where the line between the controllable and noncontrollable factors is not always clear. You can make the perfect mechanical stroke, and still miss a putt. You can make a great swing, and the wind can suddenly gust and blow your ball off-line. You can be thinking well and swinging well, and still not score well. Conversely, you can hit the ball poorly, get favorable bounces, and score well. These idiosyncrasies and fluctuations are built into the game, but, of course, they are built into all sports, aren't they? As a consequence, it isn't always easy to accurately determine when we are responsible for the scores we produce.

Everyone interprets their view of the game from their own foundation. Golfers on the PGA Tour are no different. Because of their years of success at the highest level, they tend to overestimate the degree of control they can exercise. While on the one hand they tend to blame themselves for things they can't control, they are also able to retain the control necessary for high confidence. Curtis Strange symbolizes a common bias of top golfers: "I always blame myself when I play badly, and credit myself when I play well. I was always the one who said it was my fault. I always kind of liked it that when I put my head on my pillow, I did it myself. You rely on yourself."

Once again, Jack Nicklaus serves as the model. I asked, "Jack, when competing in a tournament, against whom are you competing: yourself, a score, the field?"

Mostly only me. I am the only one I can control. They will ask me, "Jack, you have a great field this week with Palmer, Player . . ." I say, "Oh, they are here playing this week? I didn't know that." Because, as a competitor trying to win the damn tournament, I couldn't care less. *I am the only one I can control. I can't control what they do.* I am here to prepare myself for this golf course to be ready to play on Thursday. I don't care what they do. I know that if I play my game, I am going to be there. Golfers who think about the field and the nonsense, the things beyond their control, that's ridiculous.

We do not have control over the behavior of those we play with, but we do have control over the degree to which we let them affect our own golf game.

words of a champion: jim furyk, 2003 u.s. open

How do you win a major championship? You stick with it. You keep believing in the possibility of your potential. And you are sure of it, even without a whole lot of evidence to support it and maybe more than a little to contradict it. Jim Furyk knew winning a major was his potential. He wasn't having an incredible stretch of winning in 2003. He had played very well, but he hadn't actually won anything. But the courage of his convictions pushed him when he arrived at Olympia Fields Country Club for the U.S. Open. That courage was a comfort in a pressure cooker. He let the press know how that steady approach led him to winning the U.S. Open. This exchange from the champion's press conference shows that sense of self-efficacy quite clearly.

Q: Fluff [Cowan, Furyk's caddie] said you were more relaxed this week than he had ever seen you. Why was that and how big a factor was that for you this week? Did you have a sense that something big was going to happen this week?

cont. on next page

cont. from previous page

JIM FURYK: Not after the first nine of my Thursday round. But coming in this week—yeah, I was pretty relaxed. I wasn't hitting the ball as well as I would have liked to on the weekend before coming here, Monday, Tuesday, not great. But every day I just kept improving, kept getting better. My whole goal was—I talked to my wife a couple of times last week, Thursday, Friday, and I talked about winning the golf tournament. And I really—I've had such a good year. I've had some confidence in my game. I really wanted to come in here, not focusing on playing well, I wanted to come in focusing on winning the golf tournament and what I needed to do to do that.

In the past at the U.S. Open, I played a bad round at Pebble Beach, I played a bad round at Southern Hills and at Bethpage, for the last three Open championships, and I let the conditions, I let the course setup, I let things bother me and I didn't play well because of it. I came in here this week knowing that I would have to improve on that if I wanted to play well this week. I felt the physical part of my game was in pretty good shape. I felt like my mental attitude has been good all year. But if I was going to improve on my play in the last three U.S. Opens, I had to have a better attitude. I was going to have to improve on my attitude, and it showed this week.

Think about the next thing you want to accomplish with your golf game. Certainly, you have to put in the

cont. on next page

cont. from previous page

work to develop your skill to a certain point. But you also have to commit to believing that the physical skills are there. Have faith in your skills and you'll have it in yourself. Let the natural ability take over, instead of letting the circumstances inhibit your skills.

the story of dave:
attributions and waggles

I had spent the early part of spring working with a talented, nationally ranked junior golfer who was struggling with his game (we'll call him Dave). Dave had spent months in a self-described "slump" and his scoring average was up five strokes from the year before. As happens with many golfers, his confidence was shot, his attitude was negative, and his enjoyment for playing and practicing golf was diminishing by the day. In a lot of ways, his attitude was no different than what you might find in the average golfer struggling with his enjoyment of the game.

The first question I asked him is the same I ask of all golfers who come to see me; it is the same question I ask when they leave after treatment is completed (when they are hopefully playing better): "Why do you think you are playing the way you are playing? What is the cause of your poor play these days?" In this case Dave was attributing his poor play to incompetent teachers, errant weather patterns, and a series of bad bounces he'd gotten in tournaments. All external attributions over which he had little control. No wonder he was feeling helpless. In his mind, the Golf Gods were orchestrating events to sabotage his game and he had no say in the matter.

Over the course of the next couple weeks I watched Dave practice and watched him compete. I played with him and modeled good thinking and listened to what he thought as he played golf. One day I visited his teaching pro, who informed me that Dave was hitting the ball inconsistently because he was getting "stuck" during his downswing.

"He swings fine when I watch him," his instructor said, "but when he goes out to practice, he goes right back to the old way."

In essence, Dave was spending his practice sessions reinforcing bad habits. The more he practiced, the more he got comfortable in a bad position. Knowing that it would take time to retread bad habits and acquire new, good habits, I suggested he rearrange his practice schedule to spend more time on his short game in order to alleviate the pressure to score with his longer clubs.

The process of improvement began with hours of hitting balls in sessions of deliberate practice, attending to the mechanics and angles of the swing, and following William James's maxims for habit development. After two months of intelligent and diligent practice, Dave finally put together a complete round of competitive golf and won his first tournament in a long time. He was thrilled, and when he came to see me he was extremely excited. He told me of all the fairways he'd hit, the putts he'd made, and the feeling of confidence that had finally returned.

As I always do when my golfers are coming out of slumps, I revisited our initial question, "Why do you think you are playing the way you are playing? What is the cause of your good play these days?" I expected him to tell me that he was now hitting the ball better because he'd spent the past two months hitting balls constantly, even when it wasn't fun to hit balls. I expected him to say that all the work and all the effort he'd put into his short game had paid off. I expected him to say that our sessions discussing habit formation, confidence, and peak performance had allowed him to make his practice time more effective. I expected to hear that he had gained an understanding of golf like never before. I was expecting internal, controllable attributions.

But as has often been the case in my life of golf, I did not get what I expected.

"I found," he began "a little waggle that I do before I hit the ball. Instead of doing this." He bounced the head of his club up and down twice vertically. "I do this," he swayed his hips back and forth horizontally. "I waggle instead of wiggle."

"And that's why you think you're playing better?" I asked in disbelief. "Because of a new waggle!"

"Yeah," he said smiling.

This instant was what we teachers call "teachable moments," and I had to capitalize. If I had let him attribute his success to a waggle, he would go looking for future waggles to fix his play. He would continue to rely on random acts of luck chancing across his golf game.

"Dave," I began, "the reason why you are playing better is because you practiced intelligently five days a week. You are playing better because your short game is better. You are playing better because you hit balls in the rain. And I tell you this Dave, because at some point in the future, you will struggle again with your golf swing. All golfers do. And when that time comes, hard work and smart practice will bail you out. You can't waggle your way through college golf and you certainly won't waggle your way onto the PGA Tour. There is no magic bullet. Improvement is the function of a strong mind, careful practice, total dedication, and fearless play. All things at which you have improved. When neither your wiggle nor your waggle are working, these are the factors you have control over. These are what will determine your ultimate success in golf."

And with that, I patted him on the shoulder and told him I was proud of his progress. "And now," I said, "go waggle your way to the practice green. Your chipping still has a ways to go."

the right attributions

What then, are the "right" attributions that golfers should make? In short, the answer is "the correct attributions." In other words, the best explanation for our successes and our failures at any endeavor are the "right" explanations for our successes and failures. The problem, however, as Sigmund Freud discussed long ago, is that failure engenders anxiety and success often breeds pride. Consequently, human beings have a tendency to provide highly inaccurate explanations for their failures in order to avoid anxiety and for their successes in order to take more credit than they rightly deserve.

DiMarco: Perspective and Attribution

Chris DiMarco talked to me about the turnaround in his game, going from barely being able to make a living to playing on a Ryder Cup team and contending for major championships. It's not the successes that he builds from, it's the acceptance of past failures.

> The biggest thing is, you have to be able to identify your faults and learn from your mistakes. Too many guys are afraid to take an honest look at themselves and why they aren't winning. I have a good friend who should have won a tournament a couple of years ago. The guy who won went out and shot 31 on the last nine to win, but my buddy shot 3 over par to lose by two shots. If he had played the last nine like he played all week, 1- or 2-under, he would have won the tournament. But he never admitted that. He would say, "I ran into a buzz saw." But he didn't run into a buzz saw. He never admitted it to himself.
>
> For me, I remember the putt I missed to lose the

International in 2001. It took me a long time to get over missing that putt. But you know what, I choked. I gagged it. If you are man enough to admit it, identify it, then you can fix it. If you don't admit it, you don't learn. Next time, my buddy won't be prepared to deal with and play with a lead. On that point, I have people tell me, "Gosh, you should have made the Ryder Cup. You got screwed." I say, "I didn't get screwed. If I finished in the top ten I would have made it. Bottom line. That's it. I had a chance. I could have hit the shots and played my way in, and I didn't. I am not waiting to be a counting stick and rely on someone else to do me a favor. I can't control those things. But I can control my play, and that's what I've got to do. Control myself and play well enough to make the team.

Fittingly, DiMarco found himself in a similar situation heading into the last weeks of the points race for the 2004 Ryder Cup team. Again, at the International, he let a weekend lead slip away. He came to the PGA the next week needing a big finish to earn his way into the top ten. DiMarco rallied on Sunday to get into a playoff. Although he didn't win in the extra holes, he was proud of the way he handled himself and the emotions down the stretch: "As poor of a feeling as I had last weekend, my feeling this weekend was very good. I felt very much in control of my game. . . . I can promise you I did not hit one shot this week that I wasn't ready to hit."

Even more important, despite the disgust of failing the week before, despite the pressure of a playoff, despite the disappointment of just falling short on the game's biggest stage, DiMarco's attitude at the end was that of the mastery golfer. Though we had never worked together before, he called me Sunday night to talk about what he could learn and how he could prepare himself to play his best. We talked every night throughout the week about his weekend fade at the International and the pressure of playing for a spot on the Ryder Cup team at the PGA Championship. I was thrilled not only with how he came through, but with how he responded to the whole experience and the gamut of emotions he felt. He told *Golf World* magazine, "My motivation was to prove myself, and I did. A lot of people pay a lot of money for drugs to have a feeling like I had out there. That is the best feeling in golf."

Finding the "right" attribution can require thoughtful introspection. We may have to admit an anxiety-inducing personal weakness as a cause for a particular failure or a reason outside ourself for a particular success. Two things are clear, however. First, only by making the right attribution for our lack of success can we hope to correctly identify the problem responsible for our failure, correct such problems, and set ourselves on the road to improved performance. Similarly, only by making the right attribution for our successful endeavors can we continue to execute the behaviors that led to our success. Clearly, golfers must always be able to, as Tiger Woods occasionally says, "keep it real."

Keeping it real is a necessary injunction in all of life's endeavors, and certainly in golf. Once one has been true to that injunction, it is equally important to remember that unstable, internal, and controllable attributions are far better than stable, external, and uncontrollable attributions. I have already explained how attributions to inborn talent or ability are invariably problematic. Luck is another dubious attribution. Take it from Thomas Jefferson himself, who observed that "I find that the harder I work, the more luck I seem to have."

It does us no service as human beings to believe that the fruits of our endeavors are fixed, at the mercy of forces outside ourselves, and beyond our control. Such beliefs are a recipe for continual surrender and resignation in the face of adversity. They gnaw at our mastery beliefs and undermine our self-efficacy. They most certainly represent the first step on the road to accepting defeat. In keeping with the theme that I have tried to maintain throughout this book, such self-defeating attributions also foster cowardice and help ensure that we will succumb to fear rather than drive that scoundrel several hundred yards dead center down the next fairway.

A Few Words on Habit

Becoming adept at golf requires a great many skills, but more than anything it requires a habitual devotion to improvement. It's the idea of *kaizen* we talked about earlier, that zest to get better even if there is no immediate reward for the effort. When you think of this kind of commitment in golf, one great champion immediately comes to mind: Ben Hogan. Hogan once said that there were not enough hours in a day to practice all the shots you'd need to play your best golf. And, in truth, those words in many ways became his motto. Curt Sampson's delightful history of golf's glorious 1960 season, *The Eternal Summer*, paints a vivid portrait of the Hogan work ethic. Hogan may have been a perfectionist, but as Sampson describes in the book, his work—or the habit of perfecting his work—was a passion. "Despite appearances," Sampson writes, "practice for Hogan was not self-flagellation;

in a way, it was not even work." As Hogan once said in *Golf Magazine*, "You hear stories about my beating my brains in practicing, but the truth is, I was enjoying myself. I couldn't wait to get up in the morning so I could go hit balls."

Hogan embraced practice to the point of habit. Because of his dedication, great shots hit under the pressure of competition would be no different than the thousands of similar shots he had hit on the practice range leading up to an event. It is that same Hoganesque passion that you see in Vijay Singh, who became the number-one golfer in the world at age forty-one, the oldest player ever to reach that height for the first time in his career. Singh's commitment can be seen in the two workouts a day he does to maintain his fitness level, but it is most visible in the three-foot-long divot lines that gouge the area of the practice range where he's been working. Grooving his long, powerful swing has come from a habitual devotion to improvement, exactly what the golfer he admires most brought to the game. Said Singh of Hogan,

> I never met the person, but I've read every book he wrote. He never stopped practicing. There is a guy who worked. He found it in the dirt. That's the way I want to be.
>
> There is a lot more satisfaction when you try to find it, and you find it yourself. . . . I just enjoy hitting good shots. I told my caddie a long time ago—I hit a shot in one tournament, it was great, just the way I want to hit it—and I told him, "If I keep doing that, I don't need to

play because it's such a great feeling." That's what I like
to do on the range. It doesn't happen but maybe a few
times in a whole session, but that's what I'm trying to
achieve.

Now, the word "habit" has been liberally sprinkled
throughout this book's pages. Aristotle wrote that "we are
what we repeatedly do. Excellence, thus, is not an act, but a
habit." No less a philosopher than a football coach, Vince
Lombardi observed that winning is habitual but that, unfortunately, so is losing. It was William James, the father of
American psychology, who first brought the concept of habit
to the forefront of psychological thinking, pointing out that
"habits are the stuff of which behavior consists."

James argued that the vast proportion of an adult's behavior consists of habitual actions learned during formative stages
of skill development. In other words, there is a time during
which our behavior is *elastic*, simply because we are in the
process of learning. Once the learning has taken place, however, our behavior hardens and we begin to operate, as it were,
on automatic pilot. Through repetition and time, habits eventually bury themselves so deeply into the coding of human
thought and behavior that they ultimately often override conscious choice. As the saying goes, we begin controlling our
habits. In time, our habits control us. The process of change
in golf is often, as David Duval and so many others will attest,
the process of changing habits.

James also argued that cognition and emotion work in a

similar fashion. We develop not only habits of action but also "habits of mind." For example, the positive concepts that we've talked about in this book—achievement goal orientations, self-efficacy beliefs, and the attributions we typically make—ultimately become habits of thinking that are developed like any habit of conduct. After a while, a person tends to think in habitual ways, feel in habitual ways, seek habitual stimulation, pursue habitual interests. Even our romantic tastes become habitual, as we come to fall for a particular "type" of person. Rather a confining description of human functioning, eh? Confining perhaps, but nonetheless true.

What this means, of course, is that as people age, they become more strongly influenced by the behaviors and inclinations that they mastered earlier on. These habitual ways of behaving exert a powerful influence on the actions in which people engage and on the success or failure they experience as a result of those actions. As a consequence, habitual behaviors are the very stuff of which the self is made. Even the fear response can be a conditioned habit. The more frequently we give in to fear, the more sensitive the trigger becomes, and consequently, the more situations produce fear.

Two important implications arise from these contentions regarding habit. First, it seems clear that it is far better, and much easier, to cultivate good habits than to try to break bad habits. For James, the critical challenge that humans faced was making their positive and adaptive behaviors, thoughts, and emotions automatic and habitual as early as possible. For golfers—in fact, for all athletes—these behaviors include the habit of keeping on top of one's game, developing one's skills, concentrating on important features of the game, working to overcome weaknesses, organizing time well, learning to block out distracting thoughts and events, and adopting a no-fear attitude toward the game of golf. According to James, when sound practices and basic behaviors and thought processes are handed over to "the effortless custody of automatism," higher powers of mind are freed to engage complex and challenging tasks. In other words, the less one has to think about ordinary matters, the more room the mind has to think about extraordinary matters. Jack Nicklaus was a strong proponent of habit, beginning with his commitment to a steady and solid routine. His habits and routines were developed on the practice range, as he wrote:

All my life I've tried to hit practice shots with great care. I try to have a clear-cut purpose in mind on every swing. I always practice as I intend to play. And I learned long ago that there is a limit to the number of shots you can hit effectively before losing your concentration on your basic objectives. I have to believe that some of the guys who virtually live on the practice tee are there because they don't have anything better to do with their time. And I have to believe they often weaken their games by letting their practice become pointless through sheer monotony or fatigue.

A second implication of the "laws of habit" is that habits are damnably and frustratingly difficult to change or break. Like the salmon who must swim upstream to spawn, golfers fighting bad habits are fighting powerful behavioral currents. Even the simplest and most innocuous habit exerts a powerful hold on us. Have you noticed how nonnative English-speaking adults typically have a nearly impossible time changing their accent? Henry Kissinger lived in the United States his entire adult life but still speaks with the same heavy German accent he developed as a youngster. Try typing "correctly" if you learned to "hunt and peck." Nearly impossible.

Golf instructors know that one of their most difficult challenges is to alter a particularly bad habit that a golfer has developed or fallen into. Indeed, after enough repetition and time, the golf swing becomes a habitual movement. Top instructors agree that helping golfers develop new swings is initially about teaching them what to do. Beyond that, the challenge becomes the process of habituation. Making the swing become an automatic process that they can easily trust is not an altogether easy enterprise. The muscle memory part of the equation requires repetition and time. The mental portion requires patience and fortitude.

It is for these reasons that golfers must be carefully on their guard in spotting habits of action and of mind that have come to play havoc with their game. It is always best, of course, to prevent a bad habit from creeping into our play or into our mind, but this is not always possible. Here is James again: "We must make automatic and habitual, as early as possible, as many useful actions as we can, and as carefully guard against the growing into ways that are likely to be disadvantageous." What is possible, then, is to be alert to these hobgoblins, capture them early, and not permit them to dominate our thinking. Similarly, it is possible to continually practice adaptive habits that will improve our game.

the repeatable golf swing

When he made it a routine to hit 5-irons to the base of a tree more than seventy years ago, Ben Hogan was the first prominent golfer to advocate the idea of the automatic and repeatable golf swing. Hogan believed that if you did something enough times the correct way, it would become automatic. Fifty years of research in psychology has proved him correct. Habits form whether we intend for them to form or not. How you perform in competition will ultimately boil down to the habits you develop in practice. For Hogan, this meant practicing each and every shot the way he wanted to play it on the course. He once said,

> While I am practicing I am also trying to develop my powers of concentration. I never just walk up and hit the ball. I am practicing and adopting habits of concentration which pay off when I play . . . Adopt a habit of concentration to the exclusion of everything else around you on

the practice tee and you will find that you are automatically following the same routine while playing a round in competition. Play each shot as if it were part of an actual round.

In fact, Hogan was such a creature of habit and slave to routine that he said his round of golf officially began the moment he pushed open the locker room door.

Careless, sloppy practice is the primary reason why so much progress in golf is *sideways* progress and not forward progress. By grooving bad habits in practice, golfers set themselves up for failure. The reason golf is so frustrating to so many people is because you can practice and actually get worse. The sad fact is that most average golfers spend hours at the driving range perfecting *flaws*. Practice in golf should always be gauged by its quality, not its quantity. Golfers who hit thirty golf balls in an intelligent manner can improve far more rapidly than golfers who measure their practice by the clock or by the sheer number of golf balls they hit.

Many golfers believe that hitting 300 balls a day or practicing for five straight hours should necessarily lead to improved scores. Truth be told, that approach does not guarantee improvement. An essential rule to remember about golf lies in the old adage that "practice does not make perfect; practice makes permanent." Repetition can be the mother of success or of failure. What you do in practice will invariably be exposed in how you play. The golfer who hits 300 balls daily, but who does so carelessly, may hit 200 balls with one swing, 50 balls with another swing, and 50 more with yet a third swing. Talk about grooving inconsistency and carelessness. On the golf course he may have an equal chance of producing any one of a number of bad swings he's rehearsed. And if he is facing a shot that means anything—which is to say that if there is any *pressure* on the shot—the body will have an even stronger tendency to fall back on automatic processes. Pressure situations are precisely when the quality of golfers' practice is revealed.

Great coaches are always aware of the importance of smart practice. Vince Lombardi observed that practice in fact does not make perfect. Only "perfect practice makes perfect." On a similar note, fighter pilots understand the critical importance of habit. I recently asked a veteran pilot with extensive combat experience how he managed to keep his concentration while having surface-to-air missiles shot at him. He didn't hesitate to tell me that it was "training" that made him successful: "Up there, you just do what you are trained to do. *You don't really think about it too much. You just do it.*" When you know that you can trust your good habit, you really don't have to think very hard about what you're doing.

When fine-tuned skills are developed in a rigorous and disciplined way, executing them in high-pressure situations becomes far easier. The quality of the performance is always equivalent to the quality of the habit that has been developed in practice.

changing habits

There is no doubt but that people have the capacity to change their behavior. Contrary to popular musings, old dogs *can* learn new tricks. Admittedly, however, it is far easier for them to learn those tricks as young pups than as old dogs. If people better understood the basic nature of habits, there would be fewer broken New Year's resolutions, failed diets, hackers, slicers, shankers, duffers, and people who quit golf out of frustration. Phrases beginning with "I wish I had . . ." would not be so common. As in most spheres of life, in the world of golf, knowledge is power. The golfer who really understands the nature of habits has a distinct advantage, which reminds me of Ben Hogan's observation: "It really cuts me up to watch some golfer sweating over his shots on the practice tee, throwing away his energy to no constructive purpose, nine times out of ten doing the same thing wrong he did years and years back when he first took up golf."

In education we are fond of the old saying that there is a very great difference between ten years' experience and one year's experience ten times.

William James offered several practical maxims about habit:

1. In acquiring a new habit, or breaking an old one, we must launch ourselves with as strong and decided an ini-

tiative as possible. No half measures are useful in the
game of habit making and breaking.

2. It is critical to never suffer an exception to occur until the
new habit is securely rooted.

3. Every opportunity must be seized to act on the new habit
we wish to create. For James, this is a matter of "will,"
and will requires the personal conviction to act in firm
and prompt and definite ways.

4. Talk is cheap. It is action that is called for.

5. It serves us well in developing good habits or breaking
bad ones to engage in challenging activities "for no other
reason than their difficulty."

This book has been about the psychology of golf. Consequently, I have focused on psychological concepts such as
goal orientations, self-efficacy beliefs, and attributions. For
this reason, let me remind and caution golfers of all levels that
psychological processes can be at their most destructive when
problematic ways of thinking and feeling become deeply habitual. As I showed earlier, lack of confidence can become a
frame of mind; ego-oriented golf can become second nature;
making external and uncontrollable attributions can become a
regularly occurring affliction.

Naturally, it is these sorts of psychological habits that I am asked to change when golfers seek my help. The process is sometimes painstaking. It is especially trying when a golfer has permitted the habit to flourish and take root by having ignored it or inappropriately framed the perceived difficulty. A combination of quick attention, self-reflection, and accurate self-perception are nearly always the best ingredients for the beginnings of a cure.

some closing thoughts and cautions

To many readers, and certainly to effective golfers, many of the suggestions and implications I have outlined throughout this book may sound like little more than psychological principles grounded in simple common sense. Of course. But permit me two observations. First, good psychology should always be allied to common sense. Second, as Voltaire wrote, common sense is not so common. It's seldom common practice. But let me go a little further. There is often a fine line between what individuals perceive as common sense and what they have been doing for years, taking for granted that their actions are grounded in common sense and in effective action. Often, these actions reflect the simple repetition of habitual behaviors long established, seldom evaluated, and never questioned.

The philosopher Bertrand Russell once observed that in

all affairs, "it's a healthy idea, now and then to hang a question mark on things you have long taken for granted." The suggestions offered above emanate from research findings in which question marks have been hung on critical psychological assumptions long taken for granted. The suggestions I offer represent the strongest answers that psychologists have been able to obtain when these assumptions have been subjected to scholarly scrutiny. As such, they merit consideration.

But let me close with a word about the danger of "formalizing" generalizations. Famed Stanford psychologist Lee Cronbach cautioned that "when we give proper weight to local conditions, any generalization is a working hypothesis, not a conclusion." By local conditions, Cronbach meant the individual and specific features of a person or situation. The suggestions I have offered, as well as those offered by any book about improving your golf game, should be taken in that light. They should not be taken as formal principles that become rules to be followed regardless of the specific situation or of your own unique personality and playing style. The pages of this book do not constitute so much a workbook as they do a written conversation. In short, there is a danger if you think of the principles of this book as a collection of one-size-fits-all recipes for successful golf. There is no formula for individual greatness. The research in motivation and self-belief that lies at the foundation of this book is offered simply as a starting point. From here, I hope a golfer can begin to seek (with some degree of confidence) the solutions to the challenges faced each day, on each golf course, with each shot.